Personal Hope Shapes Career Progression

Joseph P. Dietrich

Abstract

Although personal hope is a concept that has received significant attention in research, little has been done to investigate the role of personal hope in career advancement. Organizational leaders are often unsuccessful in reaching, or being effective at, senior leadership levels. Concepts that differentiate organizational leaders are important to the field of organizational leadership. This study focused on the role of personal hope in helping leaders successfully advance in organizations. This study used a qualitative approach in interviewing 12 senior level leaders in the selected, global, for-profit organization. The 10 interview questions helped explore personal descriptions of the understanding and experience of hope, particularly its role in influencing the beliefs, attitudes, and behaviors of organizational leaders. The results of this study indicated that hope can be increased or decreased and is positively influenced by supportive contexts and relationships. Also, that it is a leadership responsibility to positively influence hope in organizational contexts through care, empathy, and shared vision and goals. Participants in this study attributed hope development to the experience of overcoming and learning from setbacks. Results also showed that hope positively influences realizing career goals or outcomes, but career advancement was not a main career goal provided by participants.

Keywords: Hope Dynamics, Support Systems, Setbacks, Career Success

Table of Contents

Chapter One: Introduction

Ballout (2009) asserted that understanding what causes some leaders to successfully progress, while others do not, is an important topic for employees and organizations. Carmeli, Shalom, and Weisberg (2007) noted there are many considerations for a leader's career advancement and emphasized that promotion decisions should focus on what an organization needs. In today's volatile organizational contexts, employers are increasingly expected to emphasize leadership skills that will help with individual and organizational adaptability to any environment (Ballout, 2009). Froman (2010) stated that organizations engage the best in employees by focusing on positive psychology concepts such as hope.

Norman, Luthans, and Luthans (2005) suggested that organizational leaders who possess and develop hope will be more successful than those who do not. Zbierowski (2014) argued that positive leadership includes the demonstration of hope. Froman (2010) described that hope helps leaders see and pursue opportunities. Hope can facilitate a positive orientation to experiences (Magaletta & Oliver, 1999). Norman et al. (2005) posited that hope provides valuable strength that has many important implications for embattled organizations in terms of effective leadership and employee performance and satisfaction.

Titone, Stefanik, McNamara (2013) asserted that hope provides capacity to set goals and overcome adversity to reach goals. Staats and Partlo (1993) asserted that hope levels differ from individual to individual. The level of an individual's hope can be increased through appropriate support (Lin, Qian, Li, & Chen, 2018). Norman et al. (2005) focused on the potential contagion nature of hope and proposed that organizational leaders who demonstrate hope could positively influence the hope of employees and organizations. Leaders with higher levels of hope positively influence hope in others (Norman et al., 2005; Snyder, 2000).

General Nature of the Problem

Disagreement about the nature of hope makes it difficult to have conceptual clarity (Ward, Griswold, Johnson, & Grahe, 2017). Helland and Winston (2005) asserted that the many aspects of hope provide rich discovery opportunities for leadership scholars. Hope is a meaningful concept for employees that is related to well-being across career stages (Hirschi, 2014). Niles, Hyung Joon, Balin, and Amundson (2010) suggested that personal hopefulness is essential for managing career development. Carifio and Rhodes (2002) asserted that more research needs to be done to continue understanding the development of hope and its influence on individuals. More recently, Marks, Çiftçi, and Lee (2018) argued that while hope has been largely explored in positive psychology research it only recently has been examined for the role it plays in personal and career development.

Ward et al. (2017) asserted that the theoretical connection between hope and the successful realization of established goals is foundational to hope research. There has been little research done on the impact of hope in the social context (Sagy & Adwan, 2006). Youssef and Luthans (2007) suggested that there is a lack of conceptual analysis and research on hope in the workplace. The concept of hope has only received minimal application to work and vocational contexts (Juntunen & Wettersten, 2006). More recently, Hirschi, Abessolo, and Froidevaux (2015) asserted that hope is an important consideration to vocational pursuits, yet how and why hope is a positive variable for career development remains unaddressed.

The Problem Statement

Bonet Loscertales (2007) defined career advancement as the individual realization of improved access to organizational resources and higher organizational status. While research has increasingly focused on the topic of career advancement, today's organizations provide fewer levels for promotions due to delayered hierarchies (Littler, Wiesner, & Dunford, 2003; Spell & Blum, 2000). Commons (2018) asserted that flattening organizational hierarchies is critical for innovation and described the characteristics of hierarchical organizations as a death knell to organizational success in this rapidly changing world. While the trend is to delayer organizational hierarchy, Zitek and Jordan (2016) noted that in flatter organizations there are fewer leadership roles. Dries (2011) argued that existing literature on career advancement focuses too little on contextual and structural factors, and instead overemphasizes individual agency.

The problem statement to be addressed was: The study of organizational leadership has not fully articulated the role of personal hope in career advancement. The research question for this study was: What role did personal hope play in the career advancement of leaders to senior levels in a selected for-profit organization? This study focused on senior leader level career advancement within the selected for-profit organization. The research for this dissertation focused on leaders at the senior career level associated with the Executive Band (EB) in the selected for-profit organization.

This study did not focus on attempting to measure hope, but to better understand the phenomenon.

Definition of Terms (Operationalization of Terms)

Hope

Luo, van Horen, Millet, and Zeelenberg (2020) suggested that because of a lack of clarity on the definition of hope it can lead to different perspectives on how to research the concept of hope. Webb (2013) noted there are over twenty-six theories of hope, with even more definitions. Hope has been conceptualized in a variety of ways (Dufalt & Martocchio, 1985). Kim, Perrewe, Kim, and Kim (2017) asserted that hope is a positive motivational state that goes beyond wishful thinking. Luo et al. (2020) asserted that hope focuses on something that is possible not an unrealistic wish. Boyatzis and McKee (2005) described hope as the expectation of good outcomes. However, hope does not necessarily mean quick results or immediate outcomes. Webb (2013) asserted that hope requires patience. For the purposes of this study, hope is understood as the personal belief that a positive outcome is possible and the desire to realize it (Luo et al, 2020).

Career Advancement

Bonet Loscertales (2007) defined career advancement as improved access to organizational resources and higher organizational status. Career advancement represents upward movement in organizational hierarchy and increasing income potential (Thurasamy, Lo, Yang Amri, & Noor, 2011). The selected for-profit organization's career bands are intended to show career progression, and to reflect increased responsibilities in moving up sequentially in career bands.

Senior Level Leaders

Senior level leaders are considered those at the Executive, Senior Executive, or Vice President career band levels. Typically, leaders at these levels have significant responsibility, manage teams (possibly global), provide leadership cross-functionally, and are expected to have demonstrated strong performance in leadership positions. EB leaders and above are also included in the organization's Annual Executive Incentive Plan (AEIP). Leaders at the EB level and above in the organization are also differentiated by increased compensation ranges and senior level leadership visibility. There are events and leadership meetings that are uniquely for those in the EB level or above. Additionally, those in the EB level or above are called on to evaluate the identification and promotion of other leaders to the EB level or above.

Delimitations

The participants that were included in the study were all employees in senior leadership positions in the selected for-profit organization. Each participant had direct reports, but a quantity of direct reports was not required. Participants may have been internally promoted to the EB level, or externally hired into the EB level. Because the population existed within one organization, and one division within the organization, the research and its potential findings may be unique to the organization and division studied.

This study was limited by its sample of leaders who were exclusively within the selected for-profit organization, so results are only be able to be specifically applied to leaders within the organization. Further, because this study gathered data from leaders at EB level, the results of the study may not be applicable to other employees at other career levels, or to employees from other businesses within the organization.

Limitations

A limitation of this study was that the research may be limited in its broader replication because of the organizational factors unique to the selected for-profit organization, and more specifically factors unique to the Digital Technology (DT) division of the organization. Data may not be consistent in or across other divisions within the organization. Career advancement opportunities are likely somewhat dependent on the organizational approach to leadership development and promotion criteria. A limitation may be the organizational structure, as career advancement opportunities and comparisons may not be easy to compare. A standard definition for hope was not provided to participants in advance of interviews. Without establishing a shared definitional clarity, respondents may have varied in the differences of understanding of what hope is and the associated behaviors.

Participating senior level leaders had a minimum of 12 years of experience with the organization. Senior level leaders with less experience with the organization may have different perspectives. All the participants in this research were mid-to-late career. This reality may have influenced the data, as how hope is understood and experienced could be partly a reflection of age or stage in life. Additionally, participants were in the United States or India. Responses may be different across other cultures or locations.

This study was conducted during a year in which the challenges and realities of the COVID-19 pandemic were being felt particularly within the industry of the for-profit organization studied. Responses may have been different if conducted in another industry or at another time. This reality may influence the data as roles and structures may have continued evolving and there may have been participants with low morale due to these challenging times for the selected organization. Additionally, the organization's industry's market conditions in response to COVID-19's impact on it may have contributed to career advancement opportunity perceptions and realities.

Assumptions Guiding the Study

There were several key assumptions of this study. One assumption was that participants would be able to recognize and transparently share personal factors that influenced career advancement. Certain promotions may have been influenced by organizational factors, rather than personal factors. An assumption of this study was that the role of hope could be identified amid other potential factors in career advancement. An assumption was that senior level leadership is a level that can be consistently defined within and across organizations. There may or may not be differentiation between senior levels related to number of employees reporting up to leaders. An assumption was that participants would be able to clearly understand and respond to the concept of hope as defined by the study. Additional research assumptions were that hope can be observable and measurable, and that hope is a relevant concept to the field of organizational leadership.

Brief Review of the Literature

Hope is a powerful, dynamic, and observable cognitive process (Garbowski, 2010; Helland & Winston, 2005). Martin (2018) described hope as intrinsic. Sucan (2019) asserted that hope is an important factor in guiding human life. Farran, Herth, and Popovich (1995) posited that hope is an essential human experience. Hope without action will lead to hopelessness (Martin, 2018), but action without hope is frivolous (Freire, 1997).

Snyder et al. (1991) described two elements of hope: agency (determination) and pathways (planning to reach goals). The components of agency and pathways are functionally inseparable (Sung, Turner, & Kaewchinda, 2013). Snyder (2002) later expanded and articulated three components in the practice of hope: goals, pathways, and agency. Snyder (2002) explained that this third component of hope (goals) was important because vague goals or unimportant goals would not justify the call to action needed for the agency and pathways components of hope. The pathways component emphasizes the ability to set challenging, but realistic goals (Kim et al., 2017). Terosky, O'Meara, and Campbell (2014) asserted that enhancing the agency component of hope fosters organizational change.

Personal hope as a motivational force in realizing goals is formed early in life (Snyder, 1994). Harvey, Novicevic, and Breland (2009) claimed that personal hope can be nurtured and developed. Duncan-Andrade (2009) asserted that hope is built through actions, feelings, and thoughts. Personal hope can be developed, like other skills, for the purposes of achieving improved outcomes and protecting against the negative effects of threats (Sung et al., 2013).

Research has shown a positive relationship between personal hope and personal growth, mental health, resiliency, and positive relations (Gallagher & Lopez, 2009; Hurley, 2004; Marques, Pais-Ribeiro, & Lopez, 2011). Rand and Cheavens (2009) claimed that individuals with higher levels of personal hope are drawn to goals that are more challenging than previously reached goals. Sung et al. (2013) described that hopeful leaders are more likely to see alternate ways to reaching goals, while more likely to demonstrate confidence and joy in the pursuit of goals.

Feldman and Dreher (2012) argued that hope can be increased within individuals, and increasing personal hope is accompanied by increased success in goal attainment. Conversely, individuals with lower levels of hope struggle to see paths to reach goals and to maintain goals (Searle & Barbuto, 2011). Hope enables individuals to rise above circumstances and failures, and to anticipate positive outcomes despite the realities of mixed emotions (Titone et al., 2013).

Carlsen, Hagen, and Mortensen (2012) acknowledged that there is a void in existing research dedicated to the concept of hope. Ward et al. (2017) asserted that hope is eminent for success to be realized, yet the concept of hope remains minimally understood. While the relationship between personal hope and personal well-being has been explored extensively, little research has been conducted to understand whether personal hope is easily influenced (Feldman & Dreher, 2012). Positive psychology literature has focused on hope as a positive concept for both individuals and organizations (Carlsen et al., 2012). However, little has been done to explore the role of personal hope as it relates to career advancement (Hirschi, 2014).

Work hope (or organizational hope) is a relatively unexplored concept and measure (Juntunen & Wettersten, 2006), with limited examination in education or career literature (Kenny, Walsh-Blair, Blustein, Bempechat, & Seltzer, 2010). Brown, Lamp, Telander, and Hacker (2013) described work hope as hope that is specific to a career context. Work hope motivates both the pursuit of, and attainment of, work success (Juntunen & Wettersten, 2006). Searle and Barbuto (2011) linked hope with work performance. Marks et al. (2018) posited that work hope plays a role in career outcomes.

Hope appears to enable the behaviors needed to realize the desired outcomes (Carlsen et al., 2012; Snyder, 2002). Lin et al (2018) posited that hope can be developed, is specific to a goal, and is a driver of employee behavior and attitude. Rego, Sousa, Marques and Pina e Cunha (2014) differentiated hopeful leaders from hopeless leaders, emphasizing that hopeful leaders explore new ideas and pathways more than hopeless leaders.

There is a strong relationship evident between work hope and achievement beliefs, and a better understanding of the influence of hope can help explain its role in career development (Kenny et al., 2010). Niles et al. (2010) described the importance of a leader's capacity to cope and strategies for negotiating in navigating career challenges and realizing career goals. Hope gives individuals faith in a worthwhile future, optimism despite challenges, and expectancy for career success (Anthis, 2014).

Kenny et al. (2010) suggested that personal hope is a powerful determinant of achievement related beliefs, beyond the realities of simply career planning. There is a close link between work satisfaction and life satisfaction, and it is important to understand motivational factors in work contexts (Juntunen & Wettersten, 2006). Career success can be understood through evaluating both objective success and subjective success (Fuller & Marler, 2009). Personal hope has been positively attributed to numerous career advancement factors, including job performance, job satisfaction, and improved outcomes despite stress or opposition (Siu, Chow, Phillips, & Lin, 2006; Snyder, 2000). Putting personal hope at the center of career advancement efforts enables leaders to develop the skills and persistence needed to remain effective in complicated and daunting global contexts and conditions (Niles et al., 2010).

Personal hope can be developed to positively impact performance, and hope can be a source of competitive advantage for organizations (Budhwar & Sparrow, 2002). Helland and Winston (2005) helped establish connections between hope and its role in organizational leadership by articulating hope as a concept that is observable, measurable, and part of leadership. Niles et al. (2010) posited that the active engagement of personal hope is essential for career advancement.

Research Methods and Procedures

To gather data for this case study, interviews were conducted with 12 senior level leaders in the selected for-profit organization's DT division. The interview questions explored each participant's personal experiences and identified the role personal hope may have played in career advancement to senior level leadership positions. This was a historical case study as it focused on participant descriptions of experiences that had taken place.

In this study, data were collected by recording audio of each interview and by capturing observations. Audio recordings were captured as voice memos on the researcher's iPhone for in-person interviews and audio recordings were captured as Microsoft Teams recorded meetings for virtual interviews. Following the interviews, the researcher transcribed the audio recordings of the interviews into Microsoft Word. The interview guide questions were designed to explore the personal meaning and influence of hope on individual leader goal attainment, particularly the goal of career advancement.

Description of the Population

The selected for-profit organization is a subsidiary business that falls under a larger for-profit corporation with multiple businesses in multiple industries. The selected for-profit organization is headquartered in Evendale, Ohio. The population for the study was comprised of organizational leaders at the EB level. The leaders included were from the organization's DT division. The DT division provides digital technology support across the business. The DT division has work locations around the world and is tasked with delivery of internal information technology needs and software and data science services.

The DT division within the organization was selected for its globally dispersed, broad, and industry-translatable skilled population of EB leaders. The DT division plays a support role across the for-profit organization, and the EB leaders in DT have a commonality of experiences in career navigation and in the services and expertise provided to the organization. The DT EB leaders were also selected due to the shared experiences, the common characteristics related to skillsets, and ease of access for the researcher. Demographic diversity was not a focus of this study. The diversity composition of the DT division's EB leadership was accepted as it was for this study's population. Leaders, whether being internally promoted to EB or externally hired into EB, all go through a leadership assessment process before being formally promoted to the EB level.

Creswell (2007) commented that the purposeful sampling strategy means that the researcher identifies individuals and sites for the research based on how these individuals or sites can "purposefully inform an understanding of the research problem and central phenomenon in the study" (p. 125). EB leaders in the selected for-profit organization were the right participants to include in this research because these individuals could potentially address the question of what helped a leader successfully transition to a senior level leadership role within the organization.

Data Collection Methods

Participants were interviewed in person when possible, or through Microsoft Teams video meetings when in-person interviews were not able to be scheduled. It was expected that each interview would be for up to ninety minutes, and in-person interviews would be held at the organization's headquarters in Evendale, OH. The Evendale, OH headquarters' campus is conveniently located for most employees located in the Cincinnati, OH area. Depending on the work locations of the participant population, interviews were also conducted remotely via Microsoft Teams. The researcher conducted all interviews.

Procedures for Data Collection

Data were collected by using the interview guide to present consistent questions to the participants. There were 10 prepared questions that were asked during the interviews. The responses to these questions and any follow-up or clarifying questions were captured by audio recording. In-person interviews were recorded as iPhone voice memo files on the researcher's iPhone. The iPhone is password protected. Interviews on Microsoft Teams were recorded using the Microsoft Teams' recording functionality. Microsoft Teams meeting invitations were sent individually to each participant. At the conclusion of each interview, the recording of the interview in Microsoft Teams was only available to the researcher and the participant. Following the in-person interviews, the data from the iPhone voice memo recordings were gathered and transcribed by the researcher into Microsoft Word. Following the Microsoft Teams' interviews, the

Microsoft Teams' recordings were transcribed into Microsoft Word. After transcription, the data were uploaded into data analysis software for analysis.

Analysis of Data

Data were gathered and input into a qualitative data analysis tool. The Computer Aided Qualitative Data Analysis Software (CAQDAS) Dedoose was used. This software helped collect, categorize, and analyze the data, presenting any themes and codes that helped drive the articulation of research findings.

Contribution to the Field of Organizational Leadership

Ludema, Wilmot, and Srivastva (1997) suggested that a vocabulary of hope should be furthered in organizational studies. Norman et al. (2005) posited that hope is a powerful concept that presents major implications for organizational contexts. Youssef and Luthans (2007) suggested that there is a lack of conceptual analysis and research on hope in the workplace. There has possibly never been a greater need for hope in organizational contexts than now (Norman et al., 2005). Kim et al. (2017), more recently, emphasized in the face of unpredictable adversity hope remains critical for individual and organizational success.

Wallis, Dollery, and Crase (2009) emphasized that a distinctive role of leaders is to facilitate the development of hope, and to help motivate the sustained commitment of organizational members to outcomes in the face of adversity. Personal hope enables leaders to find alternative pathways and overcome obstacles and stressors (Avey, Reichard, Luthans, & Mhatre, 2011). Hopeful leaders produce better outcomes, and positively influence employee satisfaction and retention compared to leaders with lower levels of personal hope (Peterson & Luthans, 2003). Savickas and Porfeli (2012) described hope as an important resource for helping leaders develop adaptive strategies, and as a resource for helping leaders take focused and refocused steps toward change goals. While there are other contributors, hope is an essential component in the process of realizing successful change (Ward & Wampler, 2010).

Summary

This chapter presented: an introduction to this study and its scope, an overview of the research method and procedures to be used, and a description of the importance of this topic to the study of organizational leadership. Key themes in this chapter were: the potential relevance of personal hope as a consideration for realizing career advancement, a brief look at existing literature on hope, an explanation of the problem being researched, and definition of the terms being used. Chapter Two will provide an extended review of the literature, focusing on what research insights and limitations contribute to the continued understanding of hope and its relevance to organizational leadership.

Chapter Two: Literature Review

Chapter One introduced the topic of the role of personal hope in the career advancement of organizational leaders while providing an overview of the focus of this study and how it was conducted. Chapter Two will further explore the existing literature on hope and will consider components of hope within the context of organizational leadership.

Despite being a significantly studied topic, there is still not consensus on a definition of hope (Luo et al., 2020). Carlsen et al. (2012) defined hope as a "complex and fundamental category of human experiencing" (p. 289) and asserted that hope has been studied from many different vantage points and fields of study. Webb (2013) posited that hope is a "socially mediated human capacity" with affective, cognitive, and behavioral dimensions (p. 397). Schumacher (2003) believed that hope is a constant to the human experience, while Snyder (2002) suggested hope is a learned or developed mindset, and therefore, not constant. Snyder (2002) looked at hope not solely as an emotion, but as a thinking process. Farran et al. (1995) described hope as a way of feeling, a way of thinking, a way of behaving, and a way of relating.

Norman et al. (2005) asserted that hope is often viewed as an abstract concept that is not only difficult to measure, but difficult to identify. Brown et al. (2013) claimed that measuring hope is difficult as the results may include components or effects of other related constructs. Shorey, Little, Snyder, Kluck, and Robitschek (2007) and Juntunen and Wettersten (2006) described the challenges of measuring hope effectively and argued that a hope measurement should include items that assess the presence of goals. Hope is a strong motivational force (Eren, 2015). Yadav and Kumar (2016) described hope as a dynamic, internal process that provides the clarity and willpower needed to overcome challenges and achieve goals. Hope is the motivation to attach oneself to positive outcomes or goals (Bruininks & Malle, 2005; Carifio & Rhodes, 2002; Magaletta & Oliver, 1999; Peterson & Byron, 2008; Toor & Ofori, 2010).

Hope helps leaders anticipate obstacles, identify goals, and develop multiple pathways for surmounting impediments (Luthans, Youssef, & Avolio, 2015). Hope can be generated and increased and represents a sustained commitment to realize desired outcomes (Prestin, 2013). Wallis et al. (2009) suggested that hope provides commitment to desired outcomes even when there is not calculable probability for success. Strauss, Niven, McClelland, and Cheung (2015) indicated that hope is cognitive capacity that can be demonstrated by one's will to succeed. Snyder (2002) compared personal hope to a rainbow, noting that both hope and rainbows draw individual's minds to seeing and believing in possibilities.

Personal hope has been associated with many positive characteristics and outcomes (Ong, Edwards, & Bergeman, 2006). Merolla (2014) described that while personal hope has many benefits, hope is not an indicator of virtue. McNulty and Fincham (2012) posited that hope is not an inherently positive or negative concept but indicated that the effectiveness of hope in influencing positive outcomes is partly dependent on the circumstances and contexts. While recognizing the different components and measurements of hope, Coduti and Schoen (2014) emphasized the importance of establishing a starting point for analyzing ways to improve an individual's level of hope.

Components of Hope

The three separate, but interrelated, components of hope are: goals, agency, and pathways (Snyder, 2002). Niles (2011) described agency as the capacity to develop and implement plans. Jaeger et al. (2017) suggested that the agency component of hope has two forms: perspectives and actions. Agency involves strategic perspectives or actions taken toward goals (Terosky et al., 2014). O'Meara, Campbell, & Terosky (2011) explained further that agency involves making meaning of situations and the behaviors or actions taken to advance personal goals in response to those situations. While Snyder (1994) argued that personal hope enables goal attainment, Feldman, Rand, and Kahle-Wrobleski (2009) contested that only the component of agency predicts goal attainment. Scioli, Ricci, Nyugen, and Scioli (2011) explained that hope is more than idle expectation as it prompts sustained commitment to action. Hope helps individuals consider possibilities in any situation and propels action (Niles, 2011). Agency thinking represents the perceptions an individual has of the personal ability to effectively pursue goals through selected pathways (Snyder, Michael, and Cheavens, 1999).

The pathways component of hope represents the self-perceived ability to generate the means to reach desired goals, or the ability to find alternate pathways when necessary (Snyder, 1994; Tong, Fredrickson, Chang, and Lim, 2010). Weingarten (2010) posited that cultivating new pathways is an ongoing exercise that develops individuals and personal hope. Snyder et al. (1999) described pathways thinking as the believed capacity to identify alternate paths to personal goals. Personal hope facilitates adaptation (Rodriguez-Hanley & Snyder, 2000).

Oettingen and Gollwitzer (2002) emphasized that the agency and pathways components of personal hope directly affect the attainment of goals but noted that questions remain regarding how personal hope thoughts specifically influence behavior. Crane (2014) argued that the agency component of hope has a greater influence on goal pursuit than the pathways component of hope. Snyder (2002) described how pathways' thinking includes considering how to link one's present to an imagined future, while agency is the capacity to use these pathways to reach desired goals. Niles (2011) noted the importance of each of the three components of hope and suggested that strategies or pathways for goal achievement are critical in providing the clarity needed to realize success. The agency and pathways components of hope both can predict goal progress (Feldman & Dreher, 2012). Research suggests that hopeful employees may be more motivated to initiate a task and are better equipped to envision alternative pathways to achieve goals (Norman et al., 2005). Hirschi (2014) described that there is a relationship between hope and: planning, decidedness, and self-efficacy.

Geraghty, Wood, and Hyland (2010) described that the agency and pathways components of hope can predict behaviors, and the relationship between the two components has been seen as additive. However, Geraghty et al. (2010) concluded that the components of hope could be dissociated. Sung et al. (2013) argued that the agency component of hope has a reciprocal relationship with skills and outcomes (where both build off each other), but the pathways component of hope does not have the same interchange with skills and outcomes. However, Day, Hanson, Maltby, Proctor, and

Wood (2010) believed the agency and pathways components of hope may contribute different, complementary outcomes.

Contrada and Goyal (2005) emphasized the interdependence of pathways thinking and agency. Agency describes a leader's determination to pursue all available pathways to accomplish desired goals (Snyder, 1994). The motivational qualities of agency energize the individual to confidently explore and pursue alternate pathways for effective goal achievement, and recognizing and engaging alternate pathways positively influences agency (Contrada & Goyal, 2005). The claims of Contrada and Goyal (2005) regarding the reciprocal relationship between agency and pathways thinking have been challenged by others. Tong et al. (2010) suggested some research has found agency is associated with feelings of hope, but not with pathways thinking. Terosky et al. (2014) described the importance of agency in organizational culture and posited that the agency component of hope positively influences career advancement.

Personal hope provides the will needed to be successful, and the adaptive strategies needed to persevere in the pursuit of goals (Yadav & Kumar, 2016). Titone et al. (2013) emphasized that personal hope can initiate and sustain meaningful change. Beal, Stavros, and Cole (2013) described the benefits of hope in openness to change, and argued that resisting change lowers personal hope which makes change less likely. Sung et al. (2013) described that the motivational attributes of personal hope can help leaders cope with, and adjust to, constant change.

Beal et al. (2013) characterized personal hope as an enduring psychological strength. Simmons, Gooty, Nelson, and Little (2009) suggested that hope represents one's mental state regarding the current situation. Hope also can positively influence an individual's ability to transition and to remain malleable to changing circumstances or situations (Ciarrochi, Parker, Kashdan, Heaven, & Barkus, 2015). Kashdan and Rottenberg (2010) posited that hope is related to psychological flexibility. Personal hope levels have been found to be related to the positive state of personal health (Titone et al., 2013).

Carlsen et al. (2012) described three pathways to hope: as an individual goal attainment, as a relational possibility, and as organizational processes. The hard work of articulating and nurturing the agency component of hope benefits individuals and can lead to organizational change (Terosky et al., 2014). Feldman and Dreher (2012) suggested that together agency and pathways thinking create the active practice of hope. Individuals experience hope through the focused interaction of agency and pathways (Snyder, 2002).

Hope and Optimism

Hope and optimism are comparable constructs that both represent stable future expectations, however, there are distinctions between the concepts (Alarcon, Bowling, & Khazon, 2013; Bailey, Eng, Frisch, & Snyder, 2007; Gallagher & Lopez, 2009). Through observation and experience, hope can be distinguished from other personality traits and psychological constructs (Alarcon et al., 2013). Ginevra and Nota (2018) described that hope and optimism are both predictors of career development. Optimism is a belief while hope finds a way to results through action (Snyder, Feldman, Taylor, Schroeder, and Adams, 2000).

Snyder et al. (1991) described optimism as a general outlook, while hope is specific. Titone et al. (2013) argued that while hope is like optimism and self-efficacy, hope is broader and a more complex concept that has greater relational implications.

Forgeard and Seligman (2012) noted the difference between realistic and unrealistic

expectations related to optimism and hope. Santilli, Marcionetti, Rochat, Rossier, and

Nota (2017) posited that hope focuses on pathways and motivation to realize desired

goals, while optimism focuses on outcome expectancy and an attitude to view situations

positively. Youssef and Luthans (2007) noted that the pathways component of hope is

what distinguishes hope from optimism.

Optimism is like the agency component of personal hope; however, the full

concept of hope is more complex than optimism due to its balance of motivation and the

development of pathways to achieve goals (Titone et al., 2013). Bailey et al. (2007)

explored how the constructs of hope and optimism predict life satisfaction and provided a

significant contribution to the understanding of how hope can impact satisfaction.

Aspinwall and Leaf (2002) posited that while hope is more complex than optimism, the

attributes of optimism are shared with the concept of hope. Hope and optimism both

provide beneficial effects in facilitating positive expectancies for the future and

supporting overall mental health (Gallagher & Lopez, 2009). Bruininks and Malle (2005)

suggested that hope is a powerful psychological asset and examined differences between

hope and other affective states such as optimism, wanting, desire, wishing, and joy.

Rand and Cheavens (2009) posited that hope is differentiated from optimism in its

greater emphasis on the role of personal agency in identifying and pursuing goals. Hope

helps individuals identify plans and act, while optimism can face limitations in simply

believing that things will work out positively regardless of actions taken (Gallagher &

Lopez, 2009). Kowalcky (2014) asserted that those without hope can become victims of external circumstances and remain inactive in favor of relying on chance or happenstance. Bryant and Cvengros (2004) shed light on the idea of hope as a future orientation and recognized that an optimistic disposition could provide stability in pursuing the desired outcomes. Alarcon et al. (2013) suggested that hopeful leaders rely on personal capability to realize desired goals, while optimistic leaders believe luck, the actions of others, of personal actions could all cause the desired future to be realized.

Strauss et al. (2015) linked hope to positive outcomes in task adaptivity and change responses, but noted that optimism does not share the same relationship to task adaptivity. Personal hope is positively related to personal well-being and negatively related to illness and anxiety (Alarcon et al., 2013). Busseri, Malinowski, and Choma (2013) suggested that optimism facilitates adaptive functioning, but characterized optimism as more a state of mind than an intentional plan or action. Hope differs from optimism in its emphasis on self-initiated actions (Gallagher & Lopez, 2009). Simmons et al. (2009) described that personal hope involves self-directed determination and the belief of internalized control in reaching realistic goals.

Context and Hope

Hope can be learned (Lopez, 2013). Yadav and Kumar (2016) asserted that hope is not a stable trait, but it changeable. Strauss et al. (2015) suggested that hope can be developed. Hope can be increased, particularly by focusing on the more tangible pathways thinking component of personal hope (Feldman & Dreher, 2012). Gallagher and Lopez (2009) suggested that hope is driven by personal agency and contexts which support. The concept of hope transcends cultures (Martin, 2018). Bishop and Willis (2014) argued that contextual factors influence the meaning and value of hope within a group or culture. Chang and Banks (2007) argued that hope is universally recognizable and consistently experienced across cultures and situational variables. Personal hope impacts performance across cultural contexts (Combs, Clapp-Smith, & Nadkarni, 2010). Weingarten (2010) described that while hope is desirable, conditions and environments present challenging realities that are rarely accommodating of personal hope. Cultures may treat individual and relational aspects of hope differently, causing how hope is valued and experienced to potentially vary when discussed across cultures (Bernardo, 2010). Chang and Banks (2007) suggested that while hope may be experienced similarly across cultures, research has not yet explained whether the agency and pathways components of hope are consistently similar within individuals from diverse cultures and backgrounds.

Froman (2010) discussed the importance of the organizational culture and workplace environment in either supporting or stifling positive emotions and concepts such as hope. Strauss et al. (2015) suggested that an emphasis on hope is beneficial to organizational cultures, particularly in the face of the unprecedented change and ambiguity confronting today's organizations. Luthans and Jensen (2002) maintained that hope is an important construct across both personal and professional domains. Across global organizations and contexts, higher levels or hope can positively influence adaptation to diverse situations and work groups (Combs et al., 2010).

Personal hope positively influences the quality of interpersonal relationships, and levels of personal hope are increased through individual and collective experiences (Merolla, 2014). While others can support and contribute to a leader's hope, the active engagement of the hope process falls on the individual (Kowalcky, 2014). Wallis et al.

(2009) demonstrated how a hope-based theory of leadership can facilitate interactive processes through which hope is developed. Personal hope is developed through social and professional experiences (Lin et al., 2018). Luthans, Avey, Avolio, Norman, and Combs (2006) asserted that the developmental nature of hope helps organizations realize improved performance and profitability.

Merolla (2014) described the benefits of hope in relational contexts, suggesting that hope positively influences relational maintenance and constructive conflict management due to hope's effect on emotional management and regulation. While hope can occur within individuals, Wilson and Ferch (2005) described the opportunities for developing hope and resilience within supportive environments. Hope is a relational concept that is developed and sustained through a supportive environment (Bishop & Willis, 2014). Stevens, Buchannan, Ferrari, Jason, and Ram (2014) emphasized that recognizing the contextual influences on hope is critical for individual goal setting. Hope is learnable, and environmental and experiential forces can be conducive or destructive to hope development in individuals (Yadav & Kumar, 2016). Personal hope helps individuals with positive interpersonal relationships and with adjusting to relational and social realities (Snyder, 1995; Snyder, 2002).

Personal hope has also been found to support positive communication practices in relationships (Merolla, 2014). Snyder et al. (2000) posited that hope begins at the personal level and can be understood as a positive expectancy of goal attainment. Wisman and Heflick (2016) described hope as the expectation and feeling that the desired future will be reached. Carlsen et al. (2012) argued that treating hope as an individual goal attainment downplays its relational dimension in goal attainment. However, to understand the relational implications of hope, it may be helpful to first understand hope as a personal dimension. While hope and leadership may both begin at the personal level, there are generative elements to each that are built on the personal dimension (Carlsen et al., 2012). Merolla (2014) posited that hopeful leaders are more likely to develop meaningful relationships. Wilson and Ferch (2005) suggested that organizational leaders need to prioritize the value of relationships to enhance individual development and organizational effectiveness.

Hope can be focused from either an individual internal perspective, or a shared, relational perspective (Du & King, 2013). Brown et al. (2013) emphasized that contextual variables can strongly influence, positively or negatively, the development of work hope. Carlsen et al. (2012) emphasized that hope in organizations should be approached as a differentiated and "future-oriented quality of experiencing" (p. 299). Hope plays a positive role in the workplace as it strengthens employees and helps organizations anticipate and engage in opportunities (Froman, 2010).

Hope and Success

Personal hope is grown through confirmation of one's abilities (Titone et al., 2013). Titone et al. (2013) commented that success in realizing goals "stimulates hopefulness, and in turn, fuels one's persistence, courage, and confidence" (p. 28), and emphasized that personal hope helps individuals overcome barriers. While hope and success may not be synonymous, Feldman et al. (2009) posited that hope "provides the cognitive foundation necessary to bring about successful goal pursuit" (p. 481).

Positive thinking helps individuals persevere, and perseverance often translates to the realization of improved or increased success (Forgeard & Seligman, 2012). Snyder

(2002) described the enduring emotional stability that high hope leaders experience regardless of threats to emotional well-being. Personal hope can help leaders feel less lonely and more equipped to interact effectively with others (Cheavens, 2000). Snyder et al. (1991) claimed that higher hope individuals set more challenging goals than lower hope people, and while both groups of people may attain goals, higher hope people are more successful due to the more challenging goals established.

Chang and Banks (2007) described that personal hope is associated with constructive goal-seeking behaviors and adaptive problem-solving skills. Oettingen and Gollwitzer (2002) emphasized that mentally contrasting the desired future with impeding reality, and mentally linking anticipated barriers with goal-directed response can help translate personal hope thoughts to hope behaviors. Leaders with higher levels of personal hope can more effectively engage in pursuing goals while avoiding negative psychological hindrances (McDavid, McDonough, & Smith, 2015).

Brown Kirschman, Johnson, Bender, and Roberts (2009) emphasized that hope can play an important role in how individuals deal with stress and use past experiences to help reach goals. Hope has been found to support and sustain employee resiliency in ways that improve employee effectiveness (Froman, 2010; Youssef & Luthans, 2007). Thakre and Mayekar (2016) linked personal hope with leader resiliency and expanded functioning.

The agency component of personal hope drives higher performance standards and outcomes as individuals stay motivated and persistent in setting and reaching lofty goals (Zhang & Fishbach, 2010). Individual and organizational performance is enhanced through an emphasis on the development of hope (Malik, 2013). Personal hope increases individual performance (Duggleby, Cooper, & Penz, 2009; Gilman, Dooley, & Florell, 2006; Searle & Barbuto, 2011; Snyder et al., 1991) and wellbeing (Richman et al., 2005). Research has shown that positive workplace emotions and work engagement are related to personal hope (Ouweneel, Le Blanc, Schaufeli, & van Wijhe, 2012). Snyder, Rand, King, Feldman, and Woodward (2002) emphasized that hope is a positive concept that produces greater outcomes and personal well-being. Personal hope has a linear relationship with self-control and well-being (Liu, Zeng, & Quan, 2018).

In a study on the impact of hope, people with high hope scores reported less psychological problems and maintained a more positive outlook concerning problems encountered in life (Carifio & Rhodes, 2002). Bryant and Cvengros (2004) provided an argument for how hope can predict coping and self-efficacy. Hope may help individuals have increased protection when facing negative life events, and hope can facilitate increased social support and relational belongingness (Davidson & Wingate, 2013). Oettingen and Gollwitzer (2002) described hope as a personal mindset that influences personal behavior and outcomes.

Gustafsson, Hassmen, and Podlog (2010) asserted that personal hope protects individuals from the harmful influences and realities of frustration, burnout, and blocked goals. Merolla (2014) noted that research on the concept of hope has helped articulate the value of hope in equipping leaders to deal with life's challenges and opportunities. Valle, Huebner and Suldo (2006) described that hope provides mental fortitude to help individuals overcome obstacles and be protected against difficult life experiences.

Youssef and Luthans (2007) studied the impact of hope on performance, work happiness, and organizational commitment. Personal hope increases satisfaction and career outcomes (Peterson & Byron, 2008). Hope positively impacts work outcomes (Simmons et al., 2009). Lin et al. (2018) indicated that individuals with higher personal hope levels will push harder to achieve higher performance. Hope influences positive career development outcomes (Sung et al., 2013). Eren (2015) suggested that personal hope positively influences career satisfaction and responsibility. Thakre and Mayekar (2016) described that the attributes of personal hope are crucial to workplace performance and success.

Brown et al. (2013) asserted that leaders with higher personal hope levels will be more successful at setting personally meaningful goals, and at persevering when obstacles arise in the pursuit of goals. Hopeful leaders proactively develop plans to successfully navigate adversity rather than allowing obstacles to hinder progress against goals and values (Kim et al., 2017). Personal hope levels are positively or negatively adjusted by the leader in response to personal success or failure in realizing established goals (Feldman et al., 2009). Coduti and Schoen (2014) posited that individuals with higher levels of personal hope more effectively accomplish goals than those with lower levels of personal hope.

Searle and Barbuto (2011) noted a positive relationship between personal hope and work performance outcomes. Wandeler and Bundick (2011) suggested that personal hope leads to improved workplace outcomes. Sung et al. (2013) and Sumsion (2007) posited that positive outcomes in career advancement are related to personal hope and the ongoing perseverance that personal hope enables. Coduti and Schoen (2014) emphasized that personal hope allows leaders to persevere and maintain healthy emotional management despite failures and circumstances and is an ability that can be developed to enable improved focus. Organizations that help leaders strengthen personal hope will increase the likelihood of adaptability and performance effectiveness (Harvey et al., 2009). Snyder et al. (1991) indicated that personal hope produces increased motivation and perseverance in individuals.

Betz, Hammond, and Multon (2005) asserted that in organizational contexts, personal hope improves goal identification and self-awareness. Hope is critical for the belief of career success (Niles, 2011). Personal hope significantly influences a leader's goals and success (Coduti & Schoen, 2014). Personal hope improves the quality and quantity of solutions for work problems (Peterson & Byron, 2008). Ciarrochi et al. (2015) indicated that hope involves initiating action and sustaining action while adjusting to any unexpected obstacles. Carlsen et al. (2012) looked at acts of hoping rather than states of hope to reflect the value of hope as an active process.

Hope and Leadership

Kouzes and Posner (2003) posited that leaders must keep hope alive in organizations. Hope is evidenced by an enduring posture of confident anticipation (Kowalcky, 2014). Chew and Ho (1994) described personal hope as an experience where the individual enjoys living in the unresolved, and the not yet reached destination. The goal setting component of hope positively influences career progression (Peila-Shuster, 2018).

Diemer and Blustein (2007) described that hope plays a role in career advancement through helping leaders remain connected to goals despite pressures or barriers. The merging of agency with career advancement goals can produce personal transformation, and this alignment between agency and goals can support the belief needed for bigger goals and more inspired actions (Terosky et al., 2014). Agency is

characterized by a panoramic awareness that influences a leader's thoughts and actions

towards positive outcomes like career advancement (Terosky et al., 2014). Archer (2000)

argued that individuals need time and space to evaluate personal agency and its role in

career advancement. The agency component of hope motivates leaders to engage in

personal advancement efforts and opportunities (Feldman & Dreher, 2012). Thakre and

Mayekar (2016) commented that hope is motivational in pursuing goals and

advancement.

Personal hope helps individuals rise above the bleak realities of current

circumstances to focus on the possibilities present for positive change (Carlsen et al.,

2012). Titone et al. (2013) noted that personal hope is an emotional experience that can

rise and fall in response to circumstances and the influence of others. Eren (2015)

indicated that hope and emotions are related. Strauss et al. (2015) posited that hope

creates an openness to change, whereas the lack of hope creates a negative resistance.

Hope exists in the comfort felt and demonstrated despite uncertainty or unsettled risk

(Chew & Ho, 1994). Snyder (1995, 2002) described positive correlations between

personal hope and problem-solving, self-esteem, and positive emotional stability; while

pointing to negative correlations between hope and negativity, anxiety, and lack of

motivation and engagement.

Organizational leaders play a pivotal role in establishing an organizational culture

that enables desired employee growth (Litano & Major, 2016). McDavid et al. (2015)

described that one's personal hope and sense of self-worth are related and interdependent

in one's identity development. Hope can positively influence an individual's perception of self-worth, and an individual's perception of self-worth can positively influence personal hope (McDavid et al., 2015); there appears to be a reciprocal relationship between self-worth and hope. Peterson and Luthans (2003) explored willpower and way-power as dimensions of hope, and indicated that these dimensions are related to positive outcomes. Hope positively influences an individual's pursuit of goals (Ciarrochi et al., 2015). The concept of hope represents the combination of motivation and focused efforts, to plan and reach goals (Snyder et al., 2000).

Personal hope produces improved psychological functioning (Chang & Banks, 2007), and the positive influence of personal hope on one's sense of self-worth can drive positive career outcomes (Marques et al., 2011). Ong et al. (2006) pointed to a positive relationship between personal hope and stress adaptation, both personally and interpersonally. Peterson and Luthans (2003) suggested that organizational leaders can help develop hope in others, and focused on the anticipation and expectation associated with hope. Organizational leaders with high hope levels positively influence the hope and adaptability of organizational members (Wallis et al., 2009).

McArthur-Blair & Cockell (2018) asserted that hope requires intentional practice, and organizational leaders should create space for the practice of hope. Jason, Stevens, and Light (2016) suggested that sense of community and trust were key factors in the experience of hope. A noteworthy feature of the concept of hope is the enduring quality of transcendence (Carlsen et al., 2012; Ludema et al., 1997). Carlsen et al. (2012) noted the generative nature of hope, and added that hope can be a disruptive force in opposing a closed stance or approach. Helland and Winston (2005) described that hope is a positive motivational state that helps contribute to organizational success. Hope is the belief that what is desired is possible (Ward & Wampler, 2010). Lopez (2013) asserted that hope is a personal choice. Yadav and Kumar (2016) indicated that hope produces creativity and provides emotional strength.

Snyder et al. (2000) emphasized that hope is goal-directed thinking, and posited that hope plays beneficial roles both before and after the appearance of a problem. Hope appears to be both a proactive and reactive response, individually or organizationally (Snyder et al., 2000). Hope shapes meaning for individuals and teams to interpret circumstances and obstacles while remaining resilient and protected against negative factors (Ong et al., 2006). Christens, Collura, and Tahir (2013) commented that hope requires the ability to distinguish between what is uncontrollable and what is controllable. Mills-Scofield (2012) posited that hope is a relevant consideration for organizational strategies and noted the ways hope can help individuals learn from failures.

Terosky et al. (2014) emphasized the importance of viewing career advancement as a narrative of how hope positively influences the realization of possibilities rather than a focus on the power and presence of constraints. Day et al. (2010) indicated that the adaptive and behavioral nature of personal hope is positively related to career achievement but noted that it is difficult to determine which facet (agency or pathways) of hope is responsible for the achievement. Di Maggio, Ginevra, Nota, Ferrari, and Soresi (2015) described that there is a correlation between hope and career adaptability.

Hirschi (2010) suggested that career adaptability predicted the stability of career aspirations. Buyukgoze-Kavas (2016) linked the personal hope of leaders to career adaptability. Personal hope is important for career success because it motivates adaptability (Savickas & Porfeli, 2012). The proactive development of hope helps leaders adapt and persevere to confidently realize career advancement goals (Sung et al., 2013). Niles (2011) suggested that the agency component of hope provides the foundation needed to effectively navigate career challenges. Hope is positively and significantly related to career satisfaction and advancement (Eren, 2015).

Hirschi (2014) emphasized that personal hope plays a key role in career advancement through its impact on focus and decidedness in career development and career advancement behaviors. Goal articulation is an important part of personal hope; a leader could embody hope, yet not successfully attach goals (Feldman et al., 2009). Webb (2013) described that hope involves the behavior of patiently taking time to realize one's desired future. Hope plays a key role in preventing problems and enhancing strengths (Snyder et al., 2000).

Avey et al. (2011) examined the relationship between personal hope and employee engagement and retention and concluded that personal hope increases retention. Snyder et al. (1999) noted that the experience of hope is subjective and is not a fixed process to reach goals but a belief in the ability to find a way to success. Hope is an important factor that influences job performance and career growth (Combs et al., 2010; Simmons et al., 2009). Personal hope is critical for career advancement because it helps with responses to adversity and with clarity on goal setting (Titone et al., 2013).

Hope Concerns

Aspinwall and Leaf (2002) expressed concerns with Snyder's model of hope: its lack of integration with related constructs and frameworks, its lack of account for the emotional aspects of hope (particularly in self-regulation), the relative absence of the potential significance of beliefs about the future and things beyond personal control, and its neglect of the interpersonal aspects of hope. Forgeard and Seligman (2012) emphasized the value of studying the relationship between positive thinking and career outcomes, particularly noting the importance of setting challenging goals rather than goals that reinforce the status quo and reduce or negate the strength possible through positive thinking.

Current hope research has been disconnected from exploring the role of emotions in the experience of personal hope (Aspinwall & Leaf, 2002). Gibson and Sanbonmatsu (2004) described that while positive thinking and optimism have many benefits, there are times when they can blind individuals to the need to disengage from unhealthy pursuits. Archer (2000) commented that there may be certain barriers that agency cannot overcome, and certain constraints may be healthy in providing boundaries or limitations to protect leaders from unhealthy pursuits or goals. Simmons et al. (2009) commented that establishing a significant link between hope and performance may be depend on the variables that are considered for the relationship between hope and performance.

Bartholomew, Scheel, and Cole (2015) indicated that hope as a construct has received some criticism due to concerns over cross-cultural applicability. Youssef and Luthans (2007) asserted that the developmental framework for positive organizational behavior should also be tested across cultures. However, little has been done to understand the full impact contextual influences have on personal hope (Stevens, et al., 2014). Budhwar and Sparrow (2002) asserted that research on hope needs to move from an ethnocentric approach to accounting for the breadth of cultural experiences and expectations.

Lopez, Snyder, and Pedrotti (2003) commented that research has shown that hope does not behave the same way across cultures. Chang and Banks (2007) described that levels of personal hope have not been measured effectively and compared consistently across individuals from different cultures. Budhwar and Sparrow (2002) stated that the relationship between personal hope and work performance has primarily been investigated in United States of America contexts. While personal hope is often associated with positive outcomes, Spitzberg and Cupach (2007) indicated that a positive mindset can prevent a leader from coming to terms with negative situations and can blind individuals to the potential damage unhealthy habits can cause. Merolla (2014) questioned whether personal hope could produce negative outcomes by reinforcing a false sense of confidence. Alarcon et al. (2013) posited that particularly high levels of personal hope could cause a leader to lose connection with reality and underestimate the significance of situational variables.

Summary

This chapter covered: a description of hope and its key attributes, an overview of the potential relevance of personal hope to the study of leadership and career advancement, a look at the contextual considerations of hope, and it set forth some key criticisms of hope research to date. Major themes from this chapter were: the three components (goals, agency, pathways) of hope that were outlined by Snyder (2002), the personal and relational effects of hope (specifically on success and career advancement), and the differentiation of hope from other leadership effectiveness influencers. Chapter Three will cover in greater detail the research methods and design for this study, connecting the established focus with the mechanics of its research treatment.

Chapter Three: Method

The research question of this study was: What role did personal hope play in the career advancement of leaders to senior levels in a selected for-profit organization? Chapter One introduced the overall problem and research question and provided a brief overview of the research method and a brief review of the literature. Chapter Two presented an overview of literature on hope, and focused on the components of hope, contextual considerations for hope, and the role of hope in realizing success. Chapter Three will describe the research method, research participant selection, and the interview questions that were used for data collection.

Selection of Method

A qualitative research approach was used for this case study. Twelve senior level leaders within the DT division of the selected for-profit organization were interviewed. In the study of social sciences, qualitative interviews are being increasingly used in research (Brinkmann & Kvale, 2014). Eyisi (2016) asserted that a qualitative research approach is more effective for a wider understanding of human behavior. A qualitative approach provides a richness in its basis for a significant description of discovery (Park & Park, 2016). Maitlis (2017) described that a qualitative approach serves the study of lived experience and how people flourish. Zarges (2016) noted the personal nature of hope and described that a qualitative research approach would provide a way to explore personal descriptions of the experience of hope.

Qualitative research is useful when exploring real-life conditions that are not easily replicated by laboratory research (Yin, 2004). Zarges (2016) suggested that using a qualitative approach helps explore individual perspectives of the lived experiences of phenomenon like hope. A qualitative research approach helps explore the meaning of leader experiences with concepts like hope (Bloomberg & Volpe, 2012). Hashemi (2019) suggested that a qualitative approach can help gain a richer picture by showing how life experiences and personal perceptions can inform each other.

Using interviews in research provides access to participant's experiences (Brinkmann & Kvale, 2014). Merriam (2009) asserted that interviewing is a helpful research approach for understanding how participants interpret behaviors, feelings, and experiences that cannot be observed. Puyvelde (2018) posited that qualitative interviews can help provide understanding of a phenomenon through listening to the facts and beliefs of participants. Brinkmann and Kvale (2014) argued that qualitative interviews provide precision in capturing meaning interpretation and clarity of description. A qualitative research approach helps in the search for truth in leadership concepts by exploring patterns (Billups, 2018). Qualitative research gives closer attention through interpretive inquiry (Creswell, 2007). The goal in using a qualitative approach for this study was to gain insights in the role of personal hope in the stories and experiences of senior level leaders within the selected for-profit organization.

Selection of Participants

The selected for-profit organization was a good organization to be used for this study because of its diverse and global workforce, its reputation for and investment in leadership development, and the robustness of the processes for evaluating and advancing leaders. As a large, global, for-profit organization, senior level leaders in this organization experience the constant pressures of growing expectations from shareholders and customers. Senior level leaders in this organization lead global teams across complex organizational structures and processes. The focus of this study matters to an environment like this organization's because senior level leaders play a key role in the success of an organization, and it is important for organizations to understand what makes leaders successful (Ballout, 2009).

The selected for-profit organization was also chosen as the organization to be used for this study due to ease of access for the researcher. To be considered for inclusion in this study, participants needed to be employees of the organization. Participants also needed to have direct reports. Participants were not selected randomly but were chosen based on specific characteristics. Participants were from the DT division of the organization. The DT division provides digital technology support across the organization. Participants needed to be in senior level leader roles in the DT division of the organization.

The DT senior level leaders are globally distributed, have shared experiences, and have common skillsets. The DT division has about 1500 employees globally, with about 15 EB leaders. Those senior leaders were approached and asked to participate in this case study. Leaders at the EB level with the organization were chosen for this study because they have advanced to a senior level of leadership.

The organization's career band levels progress from Hourly, OtherSal, PB, LPB, SPB, EB, SEB, VP, and Officers of the Company. This study explored the attainment of the specific goal of career advancement and particularly looked at how personal hope may have influenced the progression to the EB level within the organization. This study focused on leaders at the EB level within the selected for-profit organization and participants needed to be at that level. Whether internally promoted or externally hired, reaching those levels involved successfully completing the organization's leadership evaluation programs. The organization is very selective about which leaders are promoted to the EB level and moving to the EB level is particularly competitive.

The organization utilizes leader identification and development programs built specifically to help review and advance those identified as potentially ready for the move into and up within the senior leader levels. The leadership assessment process typically occurs once a year. In 2018, there were only about thirty candidates who went through the assessment process, out of the total organizational employee population of over 50,000. Partly in response to the impact of the COVID-19 pandemic on the organization's industry, the organization has declined to about 40,000 employees. In 2021, there has not yet been an assessment process cycle due to the organization's response to the COVID-19 pandemic and its reprioritization of focus areas considering the impacts of the pandemic on the organization and the industries in which the organization's businesses operate.

Instrumentation

A qualitative research method was used for this study. There were 12 senior level leaders in the selected for-profit organization that were interviewed for this case study. To gather qualitative responses from research participants, one-on-one interviews with open-ended questions were conducted. The interviews were recorded through audio and video recordings when not conducted in person. To help with clarity of interview questions, participants were informed in advance of the interviews that this study was related to the topic of hope in the organizational context. Depending on participant responses, there were additional follow-up questions posed to ensure clarity around participant responses.

Development of Questions

The interview questions that were used reflected the scope of this study's focus, while continuing to build on relevant research. The prepared questions asked about participants' experiences, perceptions, and beliefs. The intent of the questions was to gain a better understanding of the role of personal hope in the career advancement of the participating leaders.

The questions used for participant interviews were informed by the themes identified in the literature that was covered in Chapter Two. The literature presented in Chapter Two showed that personal hope equips leaders to overcome obstacles (Brown et al., 2013; Valle et al., 2006), involves the belief of internalized control in reaching goals (Simmons et al., 2009), influences behaviors and outcomes (Oettingen & Gollwitzer, 2002; Peterson & Luthans, 2003; Wallis et al., 2009), and includes the belief that the desired future will be achieved (Wisman & Heflick, 2016).

The following questions were used to gather insights related to the role of personal hope in the career advancement of leaders to senior levels in the selected for-profit organization. In advance of participant interviews, the researcher informed each participant that the interview questions were related to hope in the organizational context, would be focused on personal experiences that had taken place, and that it was understandable that participants may or may not have had experiences in question.

Interview Questions

1. How long have you been with this organization?

2. When you began this career, what was your goal for career advancement?

3. What has helped you remain focused on realizing professional goals?

4. To what do you most attribute having reached the senior leadership level?

5. Please tell me about a professional setback you experienced, if any, that helped you become more effective as a leader.

6. What role did personal hope play in your perseverance through professional challenges?

7. What are your beliefs about personal hope?

8. What are your beliefs about whether hope can be learned?

9. How has personal hope influenced your leadership behaviors?

10. What affect has personal hope had in your relationships with others in your work environment?

Question 1 was asked to help provide some context for participant responses based on longevity of experience with the organization. Questions 2-4 focused on professional goals and factors that contributed to realizing desired outcomes. Questions 5-6 explored personal experiences in engaging with and learning from adversity. Questions 7-8 explored participant beliefs and understanding of personal hope. Questions 9-10 focused on participant beliefs around internal and external factors and locus of control related to influence and career advancement outcomes. There may be other variables that contributed to the career advancement of the participants to senior leadership. Other possible variables are acknowledged and specified in Chapter Four of this study if identified by participants during interviews.

The interview questions further explored themes that were presented in Chapter Two. Literature in Chapter Two emphasized the role of personal hope in overcoming obstacles, internal determination, influencing behaviors, and in having a positive belief of future success. Valle et al. (2006) asserted that hope provides mental fortitude for overcoming obstacles, and Brown et al. (2013) described that personal hope helps leaders persevere when obstacles arise.

Hope is a dynamic process that provides internal willpower (Yadav & Kumar, 2016). Snyder (1994) noted that the agency component of personal hope describes a leader's determination. Oettingen and Gollwitzer (2002) suggested that personal hope influences behavior and outcomes, and Peila-Shuster (2018) posited that personal hope positively influences career advancement. Personal hope can be understood as a positive expectancy of goal attainment (Snyder et al., 2000), and hope is positively and significantly related to career progression (Eren, 2015) and hope is critical for the belief of career success (Niles, 2011).

Procedure

Interviews with participants were conducted in-person when location and availability allowed. When in-person scheduling was not possible, interviews were conducted through Microsoft Teams video meetings. In-person interviews were held in Evendale, OH, in a designated conference room or in the participant's work office. For in-person interviews, the physical location of the interviews was based on locational convenience for participants when possible.

Interviews were scheduled through Microsoft Outlook calendar invites sent from the researcher to the identified participant. Explanation was given to participants through the body of the calendar invite specifying the reason for the request and noting that the interview questions were related to the topic of hope in the organizational context. The invitation specified whether the interview would be in person or through Microsoft Teams. Interviews were scheduled for up to ninety minutes with each participant. There were 10 prepared questions that were asked each participant and follow up questions were asked as appropriate to ensure clarity on participant responses.

There was time given at the beginning of each interview for the researcher to explain the purpose of this study and to describe the process that would be followed for the interview and for the post-interview steps of compiling, analyzing, and sharing overall data. Each participant was informed of the steps that would be taken to preserve participant data privacy. Data privacy was kept by de-identifying participant responses in Chapter Four. Additionally, only the researcher has the saved video and audio files of the interviews. All documents and recordings gathered in the interview process were password protected on the researcher's laptop for protection.

Interviews were recorded using the researcher's cell phone's voice memo function for in-person interviews or were recorded on the researcher's laptop through the Microsoft Teams recording functionality for interviews not conducted in person. Additionally, during the interview the researcher took some notes in Microsoft Word as needed for purposes of accurately capturing the responses. After an interview was completed, the interview recording was transferred from Microsoft Teams recording or cell phone voice memo files and was saved securely on the researcher's laptop.

Data from audio recordings (from Microsoft Teams and iPhone recorded files) of the interviews were transcribed into Microsoft Word and saved as protected files on the researcher's laptop. The recorded files were saved securely through the laptop's password encrypted login requirement. Typed notes from the researcher gathered after the interviews were also saved in Microsoft Word as protected files on the researcher's laptop. Following the compiling of interview notes and audio transcriptions, the researcher input the Microsoft Word content into the Dedoose software tool for analysis.

Data Analysis

The gathered research data were entered in the cloud-based software tool Dedoose. To use Dedoose, the user did not need to download software, the user just needed to have access to the internet and a web browser. After setting up a new project in Dedoose for this study, the researcher imported the transcribed interviews. To transfer the compiled interview data into Dedoose, the researcher can simply import the documents into Dedoose through the clicking of a button (Dedoose, n.d.). After importing the files, Dedoose descriptors enabled a way to link participant responses to that individual to ensure preservation of response source without giving up privacy of participant. Participant identifiers were not input into Dedoose.

Once input into Dedoose, the tool was able to help automate the process of assessing participant responses for similarities and differences in words used and was able to help identify categories of themes from participant responses. The Dedoose tool was used to analyze participant responses and explore data insights. The Dedoose tool provides a secure way to manage participant data and is designed for analyzing qualitative and mixed methods research (Dedoose, n.d.). The Dedoose tool provides interactive visualizations and analytics that enables better pattern discovery and insights into underlying data (Dedoose, n.d.).

Dedoose provides great features for coding, marking up, and tagging data and has powerful visualization functionality that help expose patterns and meaning behind data visualizations (Dedoose, n.d.). Dedoose helped look for consistent words and themes that emerged from participant responses to the interview questions. In hearing and analyzing the personal stories of senior level leaders through one-on-one interviews, a software tool like Dedoose helped create a more objective and expansive approach to data mining. Repeated words and phrases were marked in Dedoose through its excerpt feature. Dedoose helps not only explore the frequency of words used by a participant and across participants, but also helps with the importance of words to the participant (Dedoose, n.d.).

Assumptions

An assumption of this study was that with the care that was taken throughout the research process and the presentation of the data, the credibility and confirmability of the study would be high. In using the same interview approach and tools for gathering data, and in using the capabilities of software like Dedoose, some of the challenges with confirmability were reduced in lessening the subjectivity of the researcher's processing of data alone. An assumption was that selected interview participants would be able to increase the understanding of the role of personal hope in advancing to senior level leadership roles in the identified for profit organization. As senior level leaders in the selected organization, these leaders lead global teams in responding to external pressures and customer opportunities.

Another assumption was that due to the reality that participants were from the same division within the same company within the same industry, and responses were collected within a specific, limited timeframe, the transferability and dependability of this study may be limited. All participants were from the DT division of the selected for-profit organization. An assumption was that there would be shared experiences and common skills for the senior leaders in DT given the support role the DT division plays for the overall selected for-profit organization. While a qualitative approach allows for a more in-depth exploration of personal stories, there were fewer participants included in using a qualitative approach. The limitations of transferability and dependability would likely present opportunities for further research.

Limitations

Due to the size of the selected for-profit organization, this study was not able to interview each senior level leader in the organization. Within the DT division, there are about 15 EB leaders. These leaders were invited to participate, but those who accepted the opportunity to participate first were prioritized and each senior level leader in DT was not interviewed. In taking a qualitative approach and using interviews to capture participant responses, that may have created challenges in participant accessibility. Calendar availability for senior level leaders can require several weeks lead time in scheduling, which may have caused a qualitative approach to be more challenging for participation. Additionally, recording the interviews may have caused participants to be less transparent in responses or details. Given the current travel and safety guidelines in place because of COVID-19, in-person interviews were not always possible. This study is not generalizable to all senior level leaders or to all for-profit organizations.

Delimitations

This study confined its qualitative interview approach to interviewing 12 senior level leaders of a global for-profit organization. Further, this study only included senior leaders in the DT division of the organization. Twelve participants represented just a small portion of senior level leaders in the overall organization. However, there were only about 15 EB leaders in the DT division. Additionally, this study was limited to participant responses to the 10 developed questions and any follow up question responses or insights. The research for this study was conducted in the year 2020. Interviews were conducted utilizing iPhone and Microsoft Teams recording functionality. Interviews only involved minimal local travel by the researcher when it was possible to conduct the interview in the Cincinnati, OH area and arrangements for in-person interview were available.

Another delimitation of this study was its focus on the role of personal hope in the career advancement of senior level leaders for the purposes of contributing to the study of organizational leadership. This study was not able to examine other topics of interest like the cultural considerations for hope, other career advancement research topics or career advancement variables, the research problem in other contexts, or the potential contribution of this study for other fields.

Summary

This chapter presented method selection and participant selection considerations. This chapter outlined the interview details and process and provided the 10 planned questions that were used during interviews with the 12 participants. This chapter also described the process that was used for data compilation and analysis following the completion of the participant interviews. Chapter Four will present the research that was conducted through interviews and analysis.

Chapter Four: Results

The problem statement to be addressed in this study was: The study of organizational leadership has not fully articulated the role of personal hope in career advancement. The research question for this study was: What role did personal hope play in the career advancement of leaders to senior levels in a selected for-profit organization? The purpose of this study was to investigate personal beliefs and experiences of hope in the context of organizational leadership. Chapter Three presented method selection and participant selections and outlined the interview details and process. Chapter Three also described the data compilation and analysis process following the completion of the 12 participant interviews.

Chapter Four will present the findings of the 12 interviews. Participant interviews were recorded and transcribed. After transcription and uploading to Dedoose's cloud-based platform, these findings were explored using the Dedoose research software to identify codes, and from the codes to understand themes in participant responses. This chapter will present the findings by sharing key themes, some of the key codes that informed the themes, and researcher observations from participant interviews.

Participants

Twelve senior level leaders from the DT division in the selected for-profit organization provided availability and accepted the invitation to participate. The other three senior level leaders were unavailable or elected not to participate. Along with the invitation to participate, the senior level leaders were informed that the focus of the study was hope in the organizational context. Participants understood that this study was on the topic of hope in the organizational context, and five (Questions 6-10) of the interview questions (Appendix A) contained the word hope. It was difficult to determine if participants would have used the word hope in their responses if the word had not already been provided for context. However, participants were not provided any definition of hope or additional context besides the interview questions and the clarity that this study was about hope in organizational contexts.

Of the 15 senior level leaders in the DT organization, 12 senior level leaders from the selected for-profit organization accepted the invitation to participate and were individually interviewed for this study. Before beginning the interviews, participants provided consent both to be included in the study and for interviews to be recorded (through audio/video means). The interviews took place over the course of three weeks. Interviews included 10 prepared questions (Appendix A). The intent of the questions was to gain a better understanding of the role of personal hope in career advancement of the participating senior level leaders. The 10 prepared questions were informed by themes identified in the literature that was covered in Chapter Two.

Years with the Organization

The first interview question asked each participant how long they had been with the organization. Many of the participating leaders had spent most of their careers with the organization, whether starting right out of college, joining through an apprentice or coop/internship program, or through an early career leadership program. Participants' years of experience with the organization ranged from 12 to 35 years, with the average number of years with the organization being 19 years. Collectively, the 12 participants had 228 years of service with the organization. Beyond years of service data, other demographic data were not collected for participants as it was not considered relevant to the focus of this study.

Stories Related to Topic

During interviews, participants shared deeply personal stories. Participant stories included the recent loss of a loved one at a young age to an aggressive cancer, a near-death motorbiking accident experience, having been born significantly premature and miraculously surviving, seeing the value of things in having grown up with little, recognizing the sacrifices their parents had made to provide opportunity to their children, and overcoming personal and professional failures. Participants suggested that, especially in a year that had been consumed with COVID-19-related industry realities and leadership challenges, hope was as relevant a topic for this organizational context as it ever has been. Participant 5 said, "If there was ever a 12-month period where your topic was relevant, this is it."

Coding

After conducting the interviews, the audio and video recordings of the interviews were transcribed into Microsoft Word using its Dictate function. After transcribing into Microsoft Word, the audio from the recordings was compared to the Microsoft Word transcription to ensure accuracy. Then the transcription documents were uploaded into the Dedoose research software. After reviewing excerpts from the interview transcriptions in the Dedoose software, codes were applied to specific words and phrases. Codes were determined by frequency and commonality in how or when participants noted those specific words and phrases.

Some of the words that frequently came up from, or were shared between, participant responses were (the frequency of those words is shown in parentheses after each word): hope (428), act (254), leader/leadership (217), see (176), team (166), good (160), learn (136), career (123), challenge/challenging (70), goal (64), hard (60), mind (53), success (37), support (35), opportunity (31), vision (31), family (30), confident/confidence (29), values (29), fail (15), faith (14), empathy/empathize (12), and risk (12). After applying the codes, they were all grouped by topic similarity, and those code groupings were all included within the four key themes that they informed.

Themes

The four key themes noted were: *hope beliefs*, *context for hope*, *the role of a leader*, and *career success*. Those themes will be presented in this chapter in that prioritized order, which was determined by frequency and commonality of key codes between participant responses and co-occurrences of key codes between key themes. Figure 1 shows how frequent words and phrases led to topic groupings that informed the four key themes.

Figure 1

Derivation of Key Themes

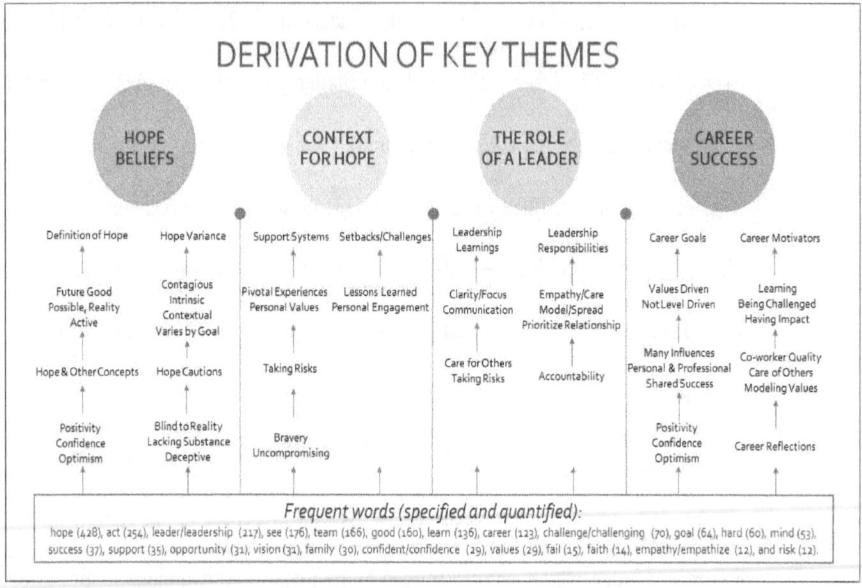

Note. Figure 1 reads from bottom to top. Frequent words and phrases were mapped by topic to derive the four key themes presented.

Some overall key observations on participant responses and participant body language and voice tone will be presented after the key themes.

Hope Beliefs

The theme identified in participant responses that will be described first is *hope beliefs*. This section will cover how participants described hope, and participant responses on the development of hope. Additionally, participant comments on hope requiring action and hope needing to be based on reality will be presented. During interviews, all participants suggested that hope can be understood in different ways and can mean a range of things to people.

Participants particularly struggled to describe beliefs on personal hope. It appeared that some of the difficulty in clearly articulating hope could have been due to not having reflected on the concept of hope as it related to organizational contexts or leadership behaviors. Within the theme of hope beliefs, participants shared their perspectives on hope definition and hope variance. In general, participants acknowledged the development of hope through overcoming and learning from challenging experiences and emphasized the importance of leadership behaviors that positively influence hope in others in organizational contexts.

Definition of Hope

Participants struggled both to define and describe the concept of hope. Participant 2 said, "I didn't think answering the definition of hope would be so difficult." There were notable pauses in responding, and some participants changed or refined responses as they thought through the interview questions. This challenge was particularly evident in responses to Question 7 (What are your beliefs about personal hope?). While participants acknowledged that having hope is a desirable thing, there was recognition that thinking through and describing hope was not something that they had done much. There was recognition, however, of the importance of clarifying how hope is defined.

Within the theme of hope beliefs, three participants (3,8,11) described hope as a future picture of something good. Descriptions of hope that were shared included a need to be able to see a desired future and being able to see oneself in that desired future. Participants indicated that hope includes a belief that there is good ahead. Participant 7 described hope this way: "a belief that things are gonna get better, things can get better, and you have the ability and strength to make it through whatever you're going through."

Participant 11 suggested that hope is always about things we do not know and involves putting faith in something we do not know.

Participant 8 described hope as a "mental construct that individuals create for themselves to get through a perceived tough patch." Those who were able to better describe the significance of learnings from experiences and relationships seemed to be able to better articulate what hope meant personally. Participants described the importance of hope in facing and overcoming hard things, taking risks, and caring deeply about others and not letting others down.

Two participants (9, 10) used the word "glimmer" in reference to hope. They explained that an individual may not need a full picture of the desired future, just a small or partial glimpse. Participant 5 noted, "You can have hope without being able to see everything ahead of you." While perfect clarity may not be necessary or possible, it was expressed that it is important that a leader have enough clarity of a desired future that they have a reason or motivation to keep pursuing the desired future. Participant 7 noted, "I think it's easy to get disillusioned…. hope is what keeps us going," and Participant 11 said, "I live on hope." In general, participants defined hope as a picture of future good, and described the importance of hope for overcoming obstacles, taking risks, and demonstrating positive leadership behaviors. Some participants articulated that hope should be realistic and oriented towards action.

Hope and Reality. Participant 1 emphasized that the substance behind hope is important. In essence, hope was described as needing to be attainable or possible. Participant 4 stated, "Hope needs to be bounded within reality." Responses indicated they felt there needs to be a path to get to the desired future or outcome. Participant 4 noted that perhaps hope is more difficult for some to model if there is not a clear path to success seen. Participant 3 described a difference between hope and a dream, noting that a dream may not have a link with reality or a path to reality.

Responses showed that participants believed hope is a good thing, however, two participants (1,8) suggested that a person or organization could take advantage of people by presenting false hope. Taking advantage of people by misrepresenting hope could involve hiding the truth or being blind to realities, whether knowingly or not. In particular, Participant 1 described that blind hope could be ignorance, and false hope could be setting a picture of the future that has no substance. In summary, respondents described hope as an attainable view of the future and emphasized that leaders have a responsibility to not misrepresent reality in leading others.

Hope and Action. Participants noted that hope requires action and suggested that personal hope takes practice. Participant 12 stated, "You learn it [hope], but then you gotta keep practicing it, otherwise you lose it." Participant 3 asserted that hope involves active engagement, not sitting back and letting things just happen. Participants 8, 9, and 12 indicated a link between hope and taking or inspiring positive action. Participant 9 stated: "I think having that hope is also important because if we didn't have a *next* that you wanted to get to you would be questioning why am I struggling so hard?" In essence, respondents asserted that hope is an action-orientated concept.

Hope and Focus. Responses indicated a possible link between hope and focus. Participants 1, 7, 10, 11, and 12 noted that because hope provides a view of the desired future, it enables aligned focus in the pursuit of that future. Participant 10 claimed, "It's very, very hard to be focused and be excellent at what you do if you don't have hope."

Other participant responses indicated the need for focus in hope, the need to nurture personal hope, and the ability to train the self in hope. In general, participants described a relationship between hope and focus.

Hope and Other Concepts. Participants offered thoughts on the difference between hope and similar concepts and struggled with the tension and clarity of how to differentiate hope from optimism, positivity, resilience, and confidence. At times, some participants used hope and optimism or hope and positivity interchangeably or synonymously. At the end of the interview, Participant 8 suggested that some of the responses provided might have been different if a different word (like optimism) was used instead of using the word hope in the interview questions. There was a link, however, in participant descriptions of the relationship between hope and confidence. Participant 1 indicated that hope and confidence go hand in hand and emphasized that it is difficult to decouple confidence from hope. Participant 10 noted that confidence and success suffer without hope. It was suggested that if leaders had hope then they had confidence, and if leaders lost hope then confidence was also lost.

Participant responses noted that hope had a lot to do with one's mindset, and one's mindset affected how a leader engaged in challenges and relationships. Participant 2 described hope as a feeling. Titone et al. (2013) posited that hope is an emotional experience that can rise or fall through experiences and relationships. Two participants (5,12) also suggested a relationship between hope and emotion or feeling. Yadav and Kumar (2016) described that hope provides emotional strength. Participant 11, however, suggested that hope goes beyond the emotional or feelings and represents an intuition, belief, or faith, which makes it difficult to observe or measure. In general, participants acknowledged ambiguity in defining components of hope. They noted that hope has a potential relationship with confidence and shares similarities with optimism and positivity.

Hope Variance

All 12 participants agreed that hope can be learned or developed. Some preferred to use words like *gained, coached,* or *influenced* instead of saying *learned*. In describing the aftermath of a personal near-death experience, Participant 11 said, "I think I learned hope when I heard my dad talking to me and telling me that 'you're gonna get through it'." Respondents indicated that hope can be increased or decreased in individuals or teams, and hope levels can vary by goal.

Team Hope. In general, participant responses indicated that an individual or collective level of hope could be influenced positively or negatively. Participant 12 noted that personal hope gives the ability to connect with others. Participant 11 suggested that hope begins personally but then extends to relationships. Participant 7 described that any team can learn hope. Participant 10 suggested that hope plays a huge role in success and hope needs to be felt and shared together within teams. In essence, participants suggested that individual hope and team hope may vary by goal and hope levels reflect both intrinsic qualities and contextual influences.

Hope Specific to Goal or Area. All participants noted that hope could be lessened or lost in a particular area or context. Participants noted that while there may be different types or contexts of hope, it is difficult to identify the separate components of hope or measure levels of hope. Participant 8, however, suggested that an individual could have high hope in one goal or part of life while having low hope in another goal or part of life. Participants acknowledged that hope can be lessened or lost and noted that if someone lost hope it could be very difficult or even impossible to get it back.

Intrinsic Versus Influenced. Participants' responses contrasted hope as an intrinsic pre-disposition, with hope being influenced by environmental factors and experiences. This contrast indicated a nature or nurture argument regarding hope beliefs and development. Participant 9 described hope as intrinsically tied to a person's identity. Participant 11 stated: "I would say hope can be nurtured but at the same time I would say hope is not something to be very logically attained." Participant 10 said, "You can maybe have some internal hope but it's so dependent on the people around you." Responses showed a lack of clarity or consensus on whether much hope could be attributed to personal identity and pre-disposition, or whether it is influenced by contextual factors and experiences. All participants acknowledged that hope can be negatively influenced by unsupportive contexts but positively influenced by supportive contexts, while noting that some hope levels may be intrinsic.

Context for Hope

The second key theme is *context for hope*. This section will present participant responses on the importance of past experiences and relationships that have informed personal development and personal hope. This section will also cover participant comments about the importance of growing through challenges for experiencing success.

Support Systems

Several participants specifically cited hope as having a contagious effect. Most participants emphasized that personal success relied on roles others have played. Leaders needed to be supported, and to support others, to realize the success that had been experienced. In general, participants suggested that hope may have reciprocal qualities. Support, both at home and at work, was identified as a critical component of career success.

In response to Question 6 (What role did personal hope play in your perseverance through professional challenges?), participant answers seemed to show that many leaders persevere because of their responsibility to personal values and relationships. Leaders suggested that due to the trust given them by others in the organization, they felt a sense of accountability to help others in the organization through the challenging situations threatening the hope of a desired future.

Participants described how instrumental relationships had been in keeping or fostering hope. Participant 10 said, "[Hope is] a feeling that you can achieve your goals, and you have the right support around you to achieve your goals." Support systems played a key role in personal success in participant responses to the interview questions. Participants told of parents, siblings, children, mentors, bosses, peers, teams, and friends all playing critical roles that have helped with personal success. In general, respondents seemed to suggest that hope is an individual variable, a team variable, and a contextual variable.

Setbacks or Challenges

There seemed to be a commonality in participants coming from lesser means, taking pay cuts, and sacrificing career stability to join the organization. Three participants (2,9,12) described starting as a coop or entry level position and working their way up over time in the organization. Participant 10 mentioned taking a significant cut in pay to join the organization. Participant 3 recounted submitting a handwritten resume to apply to work for this organization and, out of 90 applicants, was one of two people selected to join the organization.

Participant 9 described having taken a huge pay cut and potential career instability by leaving a stable job to start with this organization as an intern. Participant 2 recalled the sacrifice of his/her parents in coming to the United States from Vietnam during wartime, while not speaking English, and with little money. Participant 12 described having gotten into the best MBA college in his/her home country, then not being able to go due to medical reasons but later starting with the organization as an apprentice instead.

Participants also described setbacks or challenges in response to the fifth interview question (Please tell me about a professional setback you experienced, if any, that helped you become more effective as a leader.). Participants were hesitant to use the word *setback*, suggesting that *challenge*, *failure*, or *learning* were potentially more fitting words. In answering the fifth question, some participants shared stories about a technical challenge, while others recounted a leadership lesson.

In the setback or challenge area, Participant 11 described underestimating the significance of team dynamics, and missed the criticality of listening to the full team and prioritizing the interests of the collective team. Participant 1 mentioned "botching the integration" in leading an acquisition's systems integration into the organization. Two participants (9, 10) noted challenging peer relationships that became professional hurdles because of the distractions those relationships became. Participants 9 and 10 indicated that they had underappreciated how important it was to prioritize and handle those challenging peer relationships appropriately.

Participant 3 described getting distracted and underperforming for a year and being transparently challenged by a caring boss to decide on whether this career was wanted or not. Participant 12 described a "complete disaster" failure in unsuccessfully integrating processes between the organization and an acquired company. Participant 7 related about prioritizing personal brand over customer and organizational needs in rushing a new website deployment before it was ready. This rushed deployment went poorly and had to be undone and redone.

Participant 4 described prioritizing family needs over promotions that involved relocation, despite being told that refusing to relocate would mean delayed career advancement opportunities. Other setback or challenge stories included leadership of a failed software deployment, feeling the career setback of starting over or taking a lower role for the pursuit of new learnings and challenges, and examples of not communicating effectively or not clarifying roles and responsibilities well to the detriment of the team or outcome.

Participants described personal learnings and strength gained from the setbacks or challenges they faced. However, to gain that learning or strength, responses indicated that it took humbly reflecting on and embracing the improvement opportunity and having the desire to continue to develop. Participant responses suggested that challenges or setbacks were not uniquely contained in the professional context, instead, personal and professional learnings were inseparable in their impact.

The setbacks or challenges, whether personal or professional, provided development opportunities, both personally and professionally. In general, participants indicated that hope could be increased through overcoming setbacks or challenges, individually or collectively. Participant 6 mentioned that overcoming obstacles and challenges requires hope and represents hope in action. All participants described how overcoming challenges or setbacks had made them better leaders.

Experiences

Participants described how past experiences and relationships provided their leadership resilience and hope in facing new setbacks or challenges. Participant 6 described having gained resilience through overcoming professional leadership challenges and mentioned that hope helped provide the persistence needed for success, "Hope does play a big role [in success]…because that's where you see the end of the light at the end of the tunnel." Participant 5 suggested that overcoming challenging experiences provided emotional resilience which grows hope, saying "When you have no lived experience, I think it's harder to have hope."

Participants also stated that past experiences provided perspective that enabled them to feel less intimidated by new challenges, given the magnitude of what had already been overcome. Some participants described being grateful for what others had done to help them be where they are today, and for the value of overcoming challenges and having meaningful relationships for shaping their leadership development. Overcoming challenging experiences and relying on strong relational support systems seemed critical to participant growth in hope.

Participants highlighted the significance of parents, family, and upbringing for informing values. Several participants mentioned coming from lesser financial means which helped them now in being grateful for having increased financial means. In those cases, this seemed to reinforce the importance of keeping perspective through reflecting on upbringing circumstances. Some participants described coming from lower middle-class upbringings, and that experience being a reminder now to them to remain grateful and to keep comparisons in perspective. Participant 4 questioned whether there are things that could cause advantage or disadvantage to people differently based largely on contextual factors.

Participants 1, 4, 5, 8, and 11 mentioned the relationship between personal faith and personal hope. Of those that mentioned this connection, Participants 4, 5, and 11 indicated that personal faith helped provide a source of hope. Personal faith provided confidence and clarity. However, participant 8 indicated that they no longer see personal faith as a source of personal hope. Participant 8 noted that, while not a religious person, religion can be a source of hope and inspiration for people. Elaborating on this, Participant 8 said, "I don't know that I have a source of hope." Participants responses suggested that hope is needed for individuals and in organizations, particularly with the challenges of living through the individual, organizational, and industry realities of a COVID-19 environment. The theme of context for hope showed the significance of experiencing, learning from, and reflecting on setbacks and support systems for leadership success.

The Role of a Leader

The third theme is *the role of a leader*. This section will share how participants described lessons learned in leadership development and the clarity gained for better understanding leadership responsibilities. Participants acknowledged that they had not reflected on the relationship between hope and leadership behaviors. Participant 4 said, "Wow. I've never thought of my leadership behaviors in the context of hope."

In reference to hope and leadership behaviors, Participant 7 stated, "This is such a shift in how I've always thought about my role." Yet, despite this, participants acknowledged the importance of hope for organizational leadership. For example, participant 8 described hope as a "bonding agent" that helps rally individuals together around a shared pursuit. While participants, in general, may not have given much thought to how hope had informed their leadership behaviors, participants acknowledged that hope is a leadership responsibility and can be demonstrated by taking risks and showing care for others.

Leadership Learnings

The senior level leaders that participated in this study had a common emphasis on prioritizing the pursuit of learning and assimilating learnings for leadership growth. The leadership learnings described produced confidence, perspective gained from past experiences, and clarity in what was most important for leading well towards a desired future. In essence, participants described being better leaders and more hopeful leaders through learning from experiences.

In describing a setback, Participant 7 said, "I think back to the black and blue mark and the scars that I have from that challenge that I lived through and how that has informed decisions now." Participant 2, however, noted that negative experiences could deteriorate hope. Participants noted that reflecting on and embracing previous leadership learnings provided resilience, strength, and mettle for navigating new challenges. In general, respondents indicated that setbacks or challenges had provided important learnings and an understanding of caring for others and taking risks.

Care for Others. A specific leadership learning was to not underestimate what those on a leader's team are going through and taking care to support them. Participant 11 shared, "[Hope] makes us more sensitive as people, so as a leader it helped me a lot develop that empathy for others." There was a recognition in participant responses of the value of listening to others, caring for others, and focusing on shared success, not just individual success.

In the stories shared by participants of professional setbacks, participants noted the importance of bringing others along as a leader. Participant 10 said, "The key thing that I learned from it was it's not always just about the work that you do…. you also need to have great relationships with your peers." There was also recognition of the importance of leaders providing clear and transparent communication to their teams to show care and help them through challenges and towards the desired future. In essence, respondents indicated that one of the learnings from overcoming challenges was the importance of demonstrating hope by caring for others.

Taking Risks. Participant 11 stated, "[Hope] also helps in risk-taking…if you analytically calculate and take risk it'll always happen to be incremental because that's what logically you'll arrive at, but hope helps us take a few leaps and trust." Participants 9 and 11 mentioned the importance that taking risks played in leadership development. All participants acknowledged the benefits of having taken risks for personal growth and career success. This included exposure to tough situations, choosing to take the hardest roles and most difficult projects, and embracing challenges despite the inherent risks.

Participants 5, 6, and 10 pointed to the significance of taking on the riskier or more challenging projects because of the benefits of what they learned from those challenges. Participant 12 said, "[Leaders] that take bigger risks have a higher probability of growing." Participants shared personal stories of feeling more comfortable taking risks given the past experiences that helped enable a more confident and brave approach to new challenges.

Leadership Responsibilities

In general, participants suggested that hope can be influenced positively or negatively by the context and by interpersonal dynamics. Through the leadership learnings shared by participants, and the definitions of hope and its contextual realities provided, specific leadership responsibilities emerged. Respondents described the role of leaders in showing empathy and fostering trust. Participants all suggested that leaders should model hope and nourish hope in others. Participant 1 said, "I think part of my job as a leader is to spread hope."

Focus on People. A shared assertion by respondents was that leaders need to build relationships across the organization and prioritize an organizational focus on people. Participants 4 and 5 mentioned the credibility gained as a leader through demonstrating vulnerability in describing past setbacks and in sharing lessons learned. Participants indicated that leaders recognize there are always options to consider and pursue and emphasized the responsibility of being aligned with their teams.

Participants described the leader responsibilities of pursuing and sharing success with others, showing empathy and care for those on their teams, and being transparent in vision and communications. Participants noted that leaders should articulate the desired future and collaboratively work to reach that desired future, with emphasis on modeling a hopeful attitude and approach and showing empathy and care for others.

Hope and Vision. Participants also indicated that hope and organizational vision go hand in hand. Participant 9 described vision as the foundation of hope. Participant 2 noted that hope involves seeing something beyond what is happening right now and wanting something better. Participant responses asserted that it is a leader's responsibility to give hope through substance in the vision and goals presented. Participant responses also suggested that leaders are accountable to not spread false hope through hiding or misrepresenting information relevant to reaching the goal. In essence, participants described hope as a leadership responsibility, and leaders can demonstrate hope by focusing on interpersonal relationships in the workplace and recognizing the need for a clear and shared vision in demonstrating and increasing hope.

Career Success

The fourth and final key theme explores participant insights on *career success*. Within this, participants described career goals and career motivators. Two of the codes identified within the career success theme, were being challenged and significant relationships. Participant responses indicated that the code *being challenged* focused on the value and demonstration of a work ethic, the mettle to take professional risks through difficult decisions and challenging roles, and the ongoing hunger for learning. Participants 1, 2, 4, 5, 6, and 9 described how their work ethic helped enable career success. Participant 3 indicated the hunger for learning helped with leadership success.

Participants shared that significant relationships at home and at work were a critical part of setting and realizing career goals. Within that, participants described the importance of professional success for financial security in individual and family situations, and the strong desire to focus on work relationships rather than personal career advancement. All participants partly attributed career success to relationships at home or relationships at work. Participant 6 shared, "It is impossible to separate your personal and professional life…your personal experiences in life help shape you as a leader and your professional experiences help shape you to be a better person at home."

Participant 10 suggested that a leader needs hope to be successful and supporting relationships play a role in influencing personal and team hope. Participant 1 described that it is a leader's responsibility to help others be successful personally and professionally. Participant 9 said hope "plays a huge role" in success and posited that people need to have hope to be successful in organizational contexts. Participant 9 added that having supportive relationships contributes to hope and success.

Beyond the importance of personal and professional relationships, there were a variety of answers provided for what had contributed to career success, including opportunity, work ethic, leadership style, personal values instilled early in life, personal persistence, an incessant focus on the team, courage in taking on challenges, the breadth and depth of personal and professional experiences, visibility to senior leaders, and proving value by taking care in what was entrusted.

Career Goals

Question 2 (When you began this career, what was your goal for career advancement?) focused on career advancement goals. Participants provided very little specificity about career advancement goals or ambitions that were held at the beginning of this career or at the time of the interviews. Participants mentioned the significance of reaching the senior leader level, but only two of them indicated that was possibly a personal career aspiration starting this career.

Participant responses suggested that personal hope related to career outcomes was not tied to career path details or career advancement clarity. Participants instead described that personal hope related to career goals was centered on working hard, having good relationships, continuous learning, and opportunities to make an impact. Participants described the importance of the goals of being challenged, learning, and working with good people. Another shared participant perspective was that career success was a shared result, including the people that helped make the success and any associated career advancement opportunities possible.

Participants did not have developed career advancement goals related to organizational level or status. Instead, participants emphasized meaning of the work and relationships along the career journey. Participants reflected pride in staying focused on personal motivators and values and remaining uncompromisingly persistent.

Career Motivators

Instead of describing levels of career advancement, participants noted that what was personally motivating was being able to learn and grow, taking on new challenges, having an impact on the business, representing values well, taking care of family or those around them, and getting to work with good people. Participants had interests in both the technical, functional expertise gained and people leadership growth. Participants 3, 6, and 12 described wanting a technical challenge as an imperative for career satisfaction, while participants 2 and 9 described being motivated by increased people leadership opportunity. Participants embraced being taken outside of what was comfortable or familiar to them to build satisfaction and impact.

Participants acknowledged pride in reaching the senior leader level, yet responses indicated that advancement was not the driving motivator in career goals or decisions.

The process of ongoing hope development was the focus of participants more than hope

associated with specific ambitions or goals. In general, respondents described the active

development of personal hope through challenging experiences and meaningful

relationships and emphasized the active role leaders should play in facilitating hope in

others through shared experiences and supportive relationships. Participants suggested

that personal hope helped with overall career outcomes. Career success was the final key

theme identified. The next section will explore overall observations from participant

interviews.

Observations

This section will cover additional insights gathered through researcher

observations during interviews, and researcher reflections in studying transcribed

interview notes. Throughout the interviews, the personal pride in how work was done

and the passion around doing it in a way that mattered to others was evident. Pride was

reflected in having overcome hard challenges and doing what they felt was right

regardless of pressures or dilemmas.

Reflection

Participants noted the challenge of introspection and the infrequency of reflection.

Participants commented that while introspection and reflection were valuable practices,

they had not commonly practiced, particularly on the role of hope. In particular,

Question 6 (What role did personal hope play in your perseverance through professional

challenges?), Question 7 (What are your beliefs about personal hope?), and Question 9

(How has personal hope influenced your leadership behaviors?), caused participants to pause and deliberately think. Those questions focused on participant beliefs on the role personal hope played in persevering, beliefs on personal hope, and how personal hope influenced leadership behaviors.

Emotion

There were certain elements of the interviews that seemed to evoke emotional responses. Participants particularly showed emotion when talking about how important it was to them to care for others and the importance of the care shown to them by others. Participants, in reflecting, seemed to appreciate the significance of supportive relationships for hope development and the relational qualities that most facilitated hope. There was great pride reflecting in both how care was shown to them and shown by them to others. Relationships were a key focus in participant responses to the interview questions and relationships were at the center of the emotional moments conveyed during the interviews. There was emotion shown in recounting stories of challenges and the support systems that helped participants not only get through those hard things but become stronger from experiencing them.

Summary

This chapter presented findings from interviews conducted with 12 senior level leaders in the selected for-profit organization. Participant responses were explored, and key codes and themes were identified and outlined. In summary, participants provided many personal examples of setbacks, career progression and learnings, and reflections on the understanding of hope and the experience of hope. Chapter Five will provide analysis of research findings, and will share conclusions and implications of this research, and the relationship of this study's findings to existing theory and research.

Chapter Five: Discussion

The problem statement to be addressed in this research was: The study of organizational leadership has not fully articulated the role of personal hope in career advancement. The research question for this study was: What role did personal hope play in the career advancement of leaders to senior levels in a selected for-profit organization? This study's purpose was to investigate personal beliefs and experiences of hope in the context of organizational leadership.

Chapter Four presented the research findings. Findings included codes identified in the transcribed interview responses, and the code groupings that informed the four key themes. Chapter Five will provide analysis of the findings from Chapter Four as it related to the purpose of this study. The chapter will also describe the relationship of the findings of this study to previous research and will present implications for practice and suggestions for further research.

Summary Overview of Results

The four key themes presented in Chapter Four were *hope beliefs, context for hope, the role of a leader,* and *career success*. The key themes will be analyzed in greater detail in the next section. Additionally, to provide perspective on the role of personal hope in career advancement, an analysis of participant responses related to the research question will be provided.

Hope is Positively Influenced by Supportive Contexts and Relationships

One of the key themes was the role of the context for hope. Participants noted that while hope has both internal and external factors, they felt strongly that context influences hope levels more. Titone et al. (2013) argued that hope is a complex concept with relational implications, and Bishop and Willis (2014) argued that hope is socially produced. The development of hope happens through interactive relationships with others. Snyder (1995, 2002) described that hope helps with positive relationships and with adjusting to relational and realities. Participants described how relationships can positively or negatively influence hope. Given the organizational culture implications, it is important for organizational leaders to emphasize the development of hope through positive organizational relationships. Respondents explained that hope can be positively or negatively influenced by others and personal hope is impacted by supportive or unsupportive contexts.

Froman (2010) asserted that the workplace environment plays an important role in either supporting or stifling hope. Organizational leaders can help foster workplace environments that support hope levels within individuals and across teams. Context refers to the environment or situation and the people that are part of that environment or situation. It is difficult, maybe impossible, to separate a description of an individual's hope from the influence of the individual's context. Participant 10 asserted that hope requires the right support for achieving goals. Supportive environments facilitate hope, while unsupportive contexts can hinder hope. Personal hope can be increased or decreased through relationships.

Participant 8 described hope as a bonding agent that unites people around a shared vision. Because context has such a significant impact on hope, it can be difficult to distinguish the personal realities of hope. This has important implications for organizations as hope is significantly influenced by context. Organizational leaders should look for leaders who have hope and spread hope. Leaders can help understand and influence hope in organizations.

Participants acknowledged that hope beliefs are influenced or potentially even formed through supportive or unsupportive contexts. Respondents indicated that hope is positively influenced by contexts and relationships that support, while hope can be negatively influenced by contexts and relationships that do not support. This suggests that organizational leaders should look to play an active, support role in nurturing the development of hope in their employees. With the emphasis on relationships and supportive environments for hope, organizational leaders could explore how to focus on the leadership and organizational characteristics that may best provide a supportive environment for hope.

Research has focused on the intrinsic motivation component of hope (Eren, 2015; Martin, 2018), but little has been done to understand the shared motivational qualities of hope. Hope has contagious qualities. The purpose of this study had specified personal hope as a focus, but respondents showed an emphasis on hope's contagious qualities and the recognition that context and relationships influence individual and collective hope.

Intrinsic Versus Influenced. One of the unresolved topics in the participant responses was the question of whether hope is an intrinsic, pre-disposition or something that is largely contextually influenced. Respondents indicated uncertainty about whether hope can be created or if hope can only be influenced. All participants suggested hope can be increased or decreased, both personal hope and team hope. Organizational leaders should focus on what is needed to nurture hope, and when and how hope levels can be determined.

Organizational leadership should look at ways to identify hope levels in individuals and in teams. This could include clarification of hope components and the development of an assessment for determining hope levels in leaders and the teams they lead. Ong et al. (2006) asserted that hope shapes meaning for individuals and teams. Additionally, organizational leaders should consider how leadership and the organizational culture can support the nurturing of hope, and what leadership behaviors or cultural norms could hinder personal or team hope. Webb (2013) described that hope has behavioral dimensions and is socially mediated.

Organizational leadership should look at formative experiences in leadership assessments and talent development initiatives. Additionally, organizational leaders should focus on the quality of relationships in the organization and the ability of leaders to influence hope in others through relationship. Respondents indicated that support systems play a critical role in the level of someone's hope and the development of hope. To increase hope, leaders can benefit from lessons learned through experiences, relational supports, and personal values. Merolla (2014) asserted that hope can be increased through individual and collective experiences. Context (environment, relationships) appears in this study to matter substantively for hope, both for individuals and for teams.

Strength and Confidence Gained through Experience. While all the senior level leaders interviewed had experienced some level of setback or challenge, the important outcome appeared to be what the leader did with that experience to advance personal development. Personal hope is influenced by a leader's response to success or failure in realizing goals (Feldman et al., 2009). Setbacks provide an opportunity to learn and develop hope. Participants noted the importance of the relationship between hope and learning.

Senior level leaders acknowledged the strength gained through enduring difficulty and learning from setbacks. Living through, and learning from, deeply formative challenges can help prepare leaders for future success. This would suggest that organizational leaders should look for the formative experiences and supportive relationships of leaders and look to create an organizational culture where diverse experiences are provided, and relationship prioritization is supported and expected. Carlsen et al. (2013) asserted that pathways to hope include relational possibility and organizational processes.

Respondents indicated hope was gained through reflection on past experiences and incorporating the learnings from them. How is hope influenced through experiences? It would be beneficial to understand what setbacks leaders have experienced and how they learned from those experiences. Confidence in looking ahead to a desired future appears to be strengthened by reflecting on these experiences. Are those who have encountered fewer or less intense challenges more prone to hope or those who have experienced more frequent or intense challenges? Or is it not about the number or intensity of challenges and more about how individuals process their experiences?

Responses suggest that the most impactful experiences for leaders were the most difficult ones.

All respondents described having setbacks and emphasized the value of the strength and perspective gained through learning from setbacks. In participant descriptions, it appeared the more difficult the experience, the more hope was increased through overcoming. The intensity or significance of the challenge a leader faces may provide an opportunity for hope to be increased, especially if a leader has a supportive context. While setbacks can be painful, learnings from setbacks can provide growth that enables further and future leader effectiveness.

Instead of looking at the successes that leaders have experienced or achieved, perhaps organizational leaders should evaluate the setbacks leaders have gone through and the ways that overcoming difficult experiences have contributed to a leader's development. Leaders are more equipped to lead others effectively when they have experienced and learned from setbacks. Leaders are better able to demonstrate hope when they have been tested and tried. One possible reason for this is because experiencing difficulty provides perspective and facilitates humility.

Hope can be increased as leaders gain strength by overcoming challenges and growing through experiences. Participant 5 emphasized that hope is influenced through experience as leaders can draw strength from the maturity and confidence gained through overcoming challenging situations. Having experiences to draw from provided a source of perspective for participants. Respondents gained hope through overcoming difficult experiences and assimilating learnings from those experiences.

Setbacks can help leaders become more effective if they learn from those setbacks. It was revealing that those who described significantly difficult experiences were most clear in their description of hope and in their articulation of the role of hope. There was also recognition of the relationship between reflection and hope. If leaders do not process experiences well and reflect on the learnings from them, it may diminish the ability to apply and share hope.

Contextual and experiential forces can be conducive or destructive to hope development (Yadav & Kumar, 2016). Organizational leaders should emphasize the value of individual and shared reflection on past learnings. This could include reflecting on the lessons learned from difficult challenges related to previous goal outcomes, or insights gained from the observing the impact of behaviors on previous outcomes. Individual and team hope can be positively or negatively influenced through how experiences are processed.

Hope Helps with Risk-taking. It was also noted that there may be a potential relationship of hope to confidence and a relationship of hope to bravery or courage. If participants' professional success required taking risks and overcoming setbacks, what is the role of bravery or courage in demonstrating hope? Not only is hope important to organizational leadership, but hope facilitates other concepts that are important to organizational leadership. Participants described that hope helps with risk-taking and confidence. Perhaps being able to reference hope gained through overcoming experiences enabled increased risk-taking confidence in risk-taking.

Participant 11 suggested that hope helps leaders take more risks due to the confidence hope gives for realizing a desired future. This potential relationship between hope, confidence, and risk-taking could be explored by investigating the role of hope in confidence development and by evaluating how an individual's hope level or development influences risk-taking. Participants asserted that hope helps with facing and overcoming difficulties, having confidence in taking risks, and with caring for others.

The Relationship of Hope with Other Concepts. There was a note of gratefulness through perspective, indicating that perhaps hope is not based on comparison to the goals or success of others. Also, perhaps hope requires humility in recognizing that the journey to the desired future is never an individual one but is a shared, interdependent journey. Du and King (2013) emphasized that hope can be focused internally and shared relationally. Participants acknowledged that their career success was made possible by supportive relationships at home and at work.

Respondents indicated perceived relationships between hope and focus and between hope and perseverance. It appeared that the journey towards the desired future matters more when individuals acknowledge where they come from, who they are because of it, and what is important to them as they move forward. It was difficult to determine whether the envisioned hope for the future can be separated from one's recognition of the past and present.

Organizational leaders should seek better understanding of how the processing of experiences influences individual hope levels. For organizations, this focus could change the factors assessed in organizational talent decisions. Organizational leaders, perhaps, should seek to better understand how the experience of overcoming setbacks and learning from them contributes to a clearer understanding of hope and a better demonstration of hope behaviors. Hope was noted as having a relationship to perseverance, confidence, focus, and humility.

It Is a Leadership Responsibility to Positively Influence Hope in Others

Another key theme from Chapter Four was the role of a leader. As noted, the participants appeared to not have reflected much on hope related to leadership or on hope in organizational contexts. In noting the importance of supportive contexts and relationships, respondents described the responsibility of leaders to positively influence hope in others by sharing a clear and realistic vision, demonstrating empathy and care, and confidently taking risks.

Organizational leaders should ensure their positional power considers the needs of others. Kowalcky (2014) described that while others can support and contribute to a leader's hope, active engagement of hope is the responsibility of the leader. It is a leader's responsibility to positively influence hope in organizations. Figure 2 shows how hope levels can vary within individuals and teams and can be influenced positively or negatively through the reciprocal relationship of context, team, and individual. Understanding how hope can be influenced and how hope levels interact is an important consideration for organizational leaders.

Figure 2

Model of Hope Dynamics

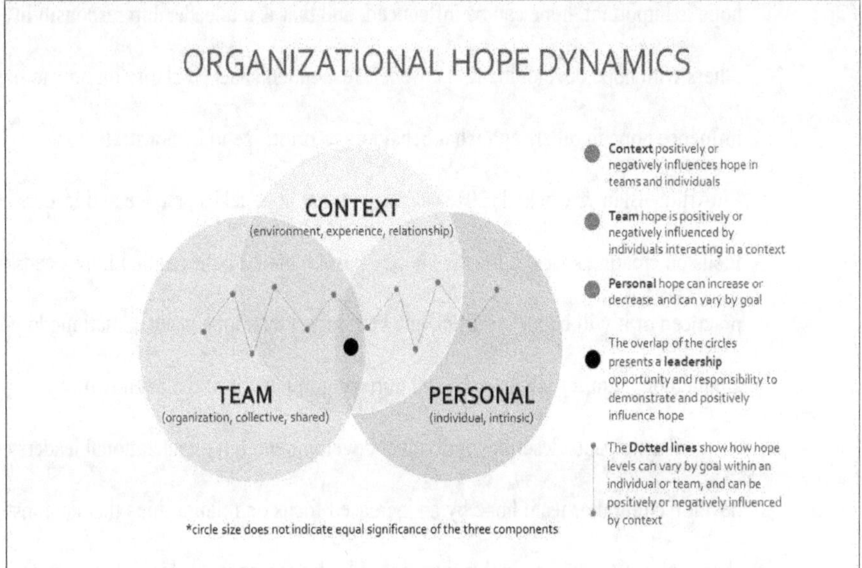

Note. Figure 2 shows potential reciprocal relationship of hope levels within and between context, team, and individual. The lines/dots reflect potential hope level variance.

This model reflects insights gained through participant responses and builds on previous research in showing how the personal, team, and contextual factors of hope interact causing potential variance in hope levels. Leaders have the responsibility to positively influence hope in others. If hope is a leadership responsibility as suggested, then leadership success can be partly determined by the role of organizational leaders in positively influencing hope in others in organizational contexts. The research question for this study focused on the outcome of career advancement. Perhaps career advancement decisions should be informed by a leader's demonstration of hope behaviors and an organizational leader's positive influence on hope in others.

Practicing Hope. Participants linked the lessons learned from past experiences in their articulation of leadership responsibilities. Respondents described that hope is good, hope is important, hope can be influenced, and that is it a leadership responsibility to help others with hope development. However, respondents lacked clarity on how to positively influence hope in others and what behaviors to prioritize to demonstrate hope. McArthur-Blair & Cockell (2018) suggested that hope takes practice and leaders should focus on creating space to practice hope. Participant 12 believed that hope needs to be practiced or it will be lost. Participant 11 asserted that hope is not something logically attained but requires taking risks and nurturing in pursuit of the unknown.

Participants described individual development, but organizational leaders could develop cultural or team hope by an increased focus on relationships that demonstrate shared hope. Organizational leaders could look to measure and improve hope levels in organizational culture through an intentional focus on hope development and the practice of hope in leaders and teams. This could include an emphasis on care, empathy, vision, transparency, vulnerability, and communication of clear and realistic goals. Demonstrating these behaviors could facilitate hope development in individuals and teams. Perhaps these behaviors facilitate general hope development which facilitates specific goal success.

Support Systems. Participants acknowledged that leader success depends on support from others at home and at work. These leaders modeled care for others and prioritized the responsibility of supporting others. While respondents struggled with answering the interview question about the role of hope in influencing leadership behaviors, they described that leaders are responsible for modeling hope and helping nurture hope in others. Organizational leaders can encourage the development of hope in their teams by showing care, empathy, and clear goals and vision. Respondents indicated that hope is contagious but may involve both intrinsic and contextual factors. For organizational leaders to develop leaders to positively influence hope in their teams, it could be useful to clarify how hope is best developed.

Recognizing that supportive contexts and relationships are important to hope development, organizational leaders can nurture supportive organizational cultures and demonstrate supportive leadership behaviors to increase hope in organizational relationships and cultures. Organizational leaders should consider the role of behaviors in influencing the organizational culture. If employees model hope behaviors it could produce a hopeful organizational culture. A focus on hope behaviors could help organizational leaders instill hope culturally beyond the influence of specific leaders.

Hope Behaviors. Respondents described the leadership responsibility of demonstrating care and empathy in modeling hope in organizational contexts and relationships. Merolla (2014) posited that hopeful leaders are more likely to develop meaningful relationships. Organizational leaders should consider how a focus on the quality of relationships and the demonstration of care and empathy can lead to successful outcomes. This focus better aligns with the career goals that were provided by participants in this study, as they described the importance of living out values, having meaningful relationships, learning, and contributing to meaningful outcomes.

Respondents also emphasized the role of leaders in sharing vision, showing empathy, listening, being vulnerable, and caring for others. Empathy was a leadership responsibility that participants described as part of hope behaviors. They indicated empathy was important for helping others through hard experiences and for building supportive relationships in shared pursuits. Perhaps an aspect of personal hope in leadership is the motivation to help the development of hope in those they lead. Organizational leaders can model hope by persevering through setbacks and collaboratively exploring options.

Focus on People. Not having clarity, admitting personal challenges, talking about humbling lessons learned, and describing the dependency on relationships for success may be less comfortable topics for leaders to discuss than describing clear and objective things like metrics, projects, and outcomes. This may reflect organizational leadership prioritization of task goals over people or behavior goals. If hope is largely influenced by context, then an implication for organizations could be that their leaders should focus more on behaviors and the needs of their employees.

Participant 10 noted that it is difficult to be focused without hope and Participant 9 indicated hope is needed for vision. Respondents noted the importance of prioritizing healthy relationships built on trust, transparency, and shared focus. They acknowledged that not only is nurturing hope a leadership responsibility, but leaders should be held accountable for supporting the development of hope in others.

Hope Accountability. Hope is important, can be learned, and is linked to successful outcomes. Organizational leadership could hold individuals and teams accountable for the demonstration of hope by clarifying hope behaviors and setting expectation for the demonstration of those behaviors. Respondents perceived the contextually and relationally dependent realities of hope. Lin et al. (2018) described that hope is developed through social and professional experiences. Participants pointed to personal hope development in overcoming setbacks and learning from experiences and relationships.

Respondents indicated that sharing hope with others is a leadership accountability. Organizational leaders could incorporate hope behaviors as a differentiator in talent evaluations and performance initiatives. This could include performance feedback and promotion criteria that emphasize the demonstration of hope behaviors. If it is a leadership responsibility and accountability to model and spread hope, then it is important that leaders understand hope, focus on hope, and demonstrate the behaviors that reflect hope.

False or Blind Hope. Organization leaders have the accountability to not spread false or blind hope by being dishonest, self-seeking, or unrealistic; nor by setting a vision that has no clarity. Participant 1 asserted that hope must have substance, and Participant 3 suggested that hope must be based in reality. Leaders should not overlook or dismiss the needs of others by using their positional power for personal benefit or preservation.

Participants described the accountability of leaders to be realistic and honest with the facts in demonstrating hope. Respondents suggested the responsibility of leaders to be honest and realistic in modeling hope. Leaders should not hide or distort things in a way that deceives others. Organizational leaders could explore a better understanding of false or blind hope and whether it is related to probability of outcomes, authenticity of behaviors, honesty of vision and communications, or motivation of actions. Organizational leaders should encourage their leaders to confront the realities of challenges and to be transparent with their teams about what it will take to achieve the desired future.

Hope and Vision. Organizational leaders can help with organizational hope by providing a clear vision of the desired future. This vision should represent what outcomes are anticipated including the desired organizational culture. Respondents described hope as requiring realistic goals, ongoing action, and ongoing development. The common saying that hope is not a strategy may be insufficient. Hope, when understood as a goal-focused, action-oriented, and supportive interaction, is a strategy. In this study, participants emphasized the ongoing process of hope development through learning from experiences and supportive relationships.

Organizational leaders can provide hope accountability through data, by looking at the presence of the goals, agency, and pathways components of hope that Snyder (2002) provided. Vision can be evaluated against the clarity of pathways and the specificity of goals. This shows the importance not only of communicating a picture of the desired future, but also of providing clear ways for incrementally measuring progress in the pursuit of that vision. Leaders should also ensure that their teams are aligned on the vision and path to reach it, while demonstrating care and empathy.

Hope Positively Influences Realizing Career Goals

As noted in this study's problem statement, the study of organizational leadership has not fully articulated the role of personal hope in career advancement. Participant responses indicated that career advancement had not been a key goal at the beginning of their careers or now. Previous research (Peterson & Byron, 2008; Searle & Barbuto, 2011; Simmons et al., 2009; Sumsion, 2007; Sung et al., 2013; Wandeler & Bundick; 2011) on hope indicated that hope positively impacts work performance and career outcomes. Participants in this study asserted that personal hope was an underlying element that facilitated positive career outcomes. While career advancement was not a particular personal focus, participants described the role of hope as an ongoing influence on positive outcomes which contributed to career success and career advancement.

Respondents also indicated that personal hope had played a significant role in professional and personal success. However, they did not specifically say that personal hope had produced career advancement. Instead, they described the significance of contexts that support hope more than the significance of personal hope. Participants described wanting to do a good job for reasons or goals other than career advancement. Respondents were motivated by personal values more than by organizational status or level.

Respondents revealed career goals that were linked to personal growth, personal values, and relationship health. They indicated that hope helps with career goals, but participants did not appear to have career advancement as a main career goal. Respondents suggested that hope helped them reach their career goals, which may have influenced career advancement outcomes, but that their hope or goal was not specific to career advancement. Participants described the ongoing development of hope through supportive relationships and overcoming challenges, and the influence of hope in career success. Hope enabled leadership development and facilitated leadership outcomes. Organizational leaders could focus less time and money on career pathing and role level differentiation if leaders are more interested in learning, challenges, and relationships.

Participants indicated other factors that had influenced leadership success and career advancement. These included both internal factors within control of the leader and external factors that a leader could not control. The range of factors provided by respondents included luck, perseverance, experiences, values, visibility, relationships, support systems, technical acumen, and timing. Considering the range of factors provided, it appears there may not be a singular recipe for career advancement. Personal and professional realities were not separated in a leader's development and success. Participants had similarities in overcoming odds, sharing success, demonstrating resilience, and caring for others. Whether envisioned in leadership level or not, hope had kept them engaged in overcoming obstacles and realizing success.

The data in this study also revealed that career goals were informed by participant values. Respondents were less concerned with career advancement outcomes and more focused on overcoming challenges and staying true to personal values. Respondents described that career motivators were not focused on position but were focused on learning, being challenged, having an impact, working with good people, taking care of others, and modeling values. Responses suggested that success is not solely an individual reality, but a reflection of the contributions of those that helped make it a shared reality.

Relationship of Present Results to Previous Research

Results in this study related to research themes presented in the literature review. Specifically, these included definitional clarity on hope, insights related to hope in organizational contexts and outcomes, and influences on hope and the impact of hope. This section will analyze the relationships of this study's results to the research presented in Chapter Two.

Context Influences Hope

Participant responses aligned with previous research (Gallagher & Lopez, 2009; Wilson & Ferch, 2005) on the belief that supportive contexts are important to hope.

Froman (2010) noted that the workplace culture can support or stifle hope, and Bishop and Willis (2014) described hope as a relational concept that is developed and sustained through a supportive environment. Participants in this study also pointed to the significance of support systems in spreading hope and the relational emphasis of hope.

Participant 10 suggested hope is dependent on supportive relationships at work and home. Brown et al. (2013) also posited that contexts can strongly influence hope development, positively or negatively. Participants emphasized hope is more contextually or relationally influenced than personally developed. This would suggest that the development of hope is not a personal endeavor but relies on supportive contexts and relationships.

Hope is a Leadership Responsibility and Accountability

Respondents noted that organizational leaders have the responsibility to nurture hope in others. This was consistent with previous research that suggested leaders need to keep hope alive in organizations (Kouzes and Posner, 2003). While noting the important of context, previous research did not appear to clearly articulate the responsibilities and accountabilities of organizational leaders in modeling hope and influencing hope in others. In general, respondents in this study indicated that it is a leadership responsibility and accountability to positively influence hope in their teams by modeling hope behaviors.

Research has noted that hope can be learned, developed, or changed (Lopez, 2013; Strauss et al, 2015; Yadav & Kumar, 2016) and individuals interviewed in this study described that hope can be influenced, learned, lost, developed, taught, or decreased. Jason et al. (2016) posited that trust and a sense of community help facilitate the experience of hope. Respondents in this study emphasized the significance of the interpersonal realities of hope. The implication for organizational leadership is that hope development is a shared phenomenon that is positively influenced through caring, collaborative, and focused relationships in the workplace.

Career Success

Research has shown that hope positively influences individual (Duggleby et al., 2009; Gilman et al., 2006; Searle & Barbuto, 2011; Snyder et al., 1991; Zhang & Fishbach, 2010) and organizational performance (Luthans et al., 2006; Malik, 2013). It was clear that the respondents in this study believed in the impact of hope on work performance outcomes. Hope plays a positive role in influencing outcomes. However, this study found that it is also important to clarify how career success is measured and to understand leader career goals.

While career advancement may not have been a clear goal for respondents, the role of personal hope was presented as having been a key factor in their success. Participants described hope more as a general process, experience, and disposition than a goal-specific enabler. Participants agreed that hope is good, hope is needed, and hope positively influences career outcomes. Respondents described the strength they gained from overcoming obstacles and leveraging lessons learned from past experiences to engage in current challenges and future opportunities. This aligns with Brown Kirschman et al.'s (2009) emphasis that hope plays an important role in helping leaders use past experiences to reach goals.

Stevens et al. (2014) noted that understanding contextual influences on hope is critical for goal setting. Participant shared career goals that centered on personal learning, being challenged, and contributing to impactful outcomes. These goals were about technical learning, challenges, and outcomes, and about leadership learnings, challenges, and outcomes. Respondents also described the career goal of having meaningful work relationships.

In this study, participants acknowledged career goals, but did not share specific goals related to career advancement. Only Participant 8 mentioned an interest in reaching the senior leader level but suggested that this was because a mentor had advised career success would be determined by whether the respondent had reached senior level leadership by 40 years of age. As Diemer and Blustein (2007) noted, hope facilitates career advancement through helping leaders stay engaged despite barriers or pressures. While respondents did not specify career advancement goals, their responses indicated that persevering through challenges and remaining true to personal values contributed to career advancement success.

Hope Beliefs

The 12 senior level leaders in this study indicated that they struggled with a clear or consistent definition of hope, yet the definitions of hope they provided reflected similarities to Snyder's (2002) components of goals, agency, and pathways. The concept of hope appeared to have received little reflection by respondents, particularly related to organizational contexts. It seemed participants struggled because they were not familiar with the topic or field of study or had not reflected specifically on an understanding, articulation, and demonstration of hope. This presents to opportunity for further research and the need to better clarify hope definition and hope behaviors for organizational contexts. To facilitate the increased development and demonstration of hope in organizational contexts, organizational leaders could focus on a clear understanding and description of attributes of hope and on clear behavioral expectations for hope.

Respondents recognized similarities between hope and related concepts like optimism, positivity, resilience, and confidence, but struggled to articulate the difference between the concepts or to agree on a definition of hope. Participants 4 and 8 acknowledged that it was particularly challenging to differentiate hope and optimism. Previous research noted the similarities of hope with optimism but argued that hope can be differentiated (Alarcon, Bowling, & Khazon, 2013; Bailey et al., 2007; Gallagher & Lopez, 2009). Research presented in Chapter Two compared hope and optimism; however, the relationship of hope and confidence was only highlighted by Titone et al. (2013) as a benefit of successfully reaching goals.

One component of hope that was noted as a difference was the action-taking aspect of hope. What distinguishes hope from similar concepts is hope's ability to identify pathways to reach the desired future and its clarity of goals and actions needed based on the options available (Luthans, Youssef, & Avolio, 2015; Snyder, 1994; Tong et al., 2010; Youssef & Luthans, 2007). Key aspects of hope that were shared by participants in this study were that hope is a possible future good that requires action to reach.

Conclusions Concerning the Findings of the Present Study

Participants indicated that they did not have specific career advancement goals at the beginning of their current career or now. Participants acknowledged wanting to be given people leadership roles and technically challenging roles, but they indicated these goals were not specific to the level of the roles in the organization. Instead, participant career goals were focused on learning, contributing, the quality of co-workers, and the quality of relationships with co-workers. Leaders of organizations could consider how this might inform what encourages employee engagement and leadership development. Organizational leaders should prioritize initiatives that are focused on organizational relationships and leader learning.

This study's results suggest that hope levels can be influenced positively or negatively and can vary within an individual or team by goal. These assertions have implications for organizational leadership as leaders can and should play an active role in influencing hope in others and demonstrating hope behaviors. Additionally, organizational leaders should ensure that there are clear goals for their teams and an appreciation for the importance of how experiences are processed, and relationships prioritized for hope development.

Rather than just focus on advancement goals, organizational leaders could spend more time on providing new challenges and learning experiences. Additionally, given the emphasis participants gave to the quality of work relationships, organizational leaders could focus more on organizational culture and leadership behavior development. Respondents indicated the importance of shared pursuits over individual activities.

Perhaps organizational leaders could put more focus on team dynamics and shared goals versus individual goals. For instance, organizational leaders could consider team goal setting rather than individual goal setting. This would involve teams collectively establishing vision and clarifying shared goals to prioritize in pursuit of the vision. This approach could change priority setting processes and performance management processes. Additionally, organizational leadership could look for feedback from a leader's team on the leader's demonstration of hope behaviors.

Conceptual clarity on hope is important to determine how to develop hope. There was consistency in participant responses on hope as something good in the future that people can act towards. There did not appear to be alignment from responses about how much of hope could be attributed to intrinsic personal disposition, personal action or development, or external influences. Participants indicated that individuals may have intrinsic hope levels, but that those hope levels can be positively or negatively influenced. Organizational leaders should communicate a definition of hope and a description of hope behaviors.

Implications for Practice

There appear to be implications for practice in organizations. Participants suggested that hope plays an important role in individual and collective success yet struggled in clearly defining hope and articulating the steps leaders should take to model hope effectively. If hope is essential, as respondents noted, then definitional clarity and operational focus are critical to giving hope the emphasis it deserves. Leaders could be better equipped to model and spread hope if centered around a consistent hope definition, model, and articulation of hope behaviors. In general, participants suggested that hope is an important personal and organizational variable. As definitional clarity and hope behaviors are specified for organizational contexts, organizational leaders can focus on efforts to enhance organizational hope for a healthy organizational culture and for realizing organizational goals. Hope is an important organizational variable that can be, and should be, cultivated by organizational leaders.

Participant descriptions of personal hope levels and the development of hope showed that individuals may have certain intrinsic pre-dispositions towards hope that impact hope levels. However, respondents suggested that hope can be, and largely is, increased or decreased through significant experiences and relationships, and how an individual responds to experiences and engages in relationships. This may suggest that while leaders can focus on the development of hope, hope is largely influenced by how a leader reflects on and incorporates learnings from experiences and the nature of a leader's relationships.

Leaders in this study acknowledged having given little reflection to hope behaviors. Reflecting on past experiences, and on how overcoming challenges developed hope, can help inform a leader's hope. To develop hope, it is important to help leaders reflect on their past experiences and consider how their past experiences and relationships help frame the understanding and practice of leadership behaviors. Organizational leadership could focus on understanding the formative experiences and learnings of leaders and look to develop supportive relationships and provide formative experiences. Organizational leaders can clarify their responsibility and accountability for demonstrating hope behaviors to positively influence individual, team, and contextual hope dynamics.

Suggestions for Future Research

Future research could explore relational or cultural hope in organizations. What are the relational qualities of hope, and how can they be supported by organizational cultures? This could include assessing which behaviors support hope development and which behaviors may stifle hope development in organizational culture. Stevens et al.

(2014) noted that little has been done to understand the impact of contextual influences on hope. Also, future research could study the role of hope in career outcomes other than career advancement, such as employee engagement, career satisfaction, people leadership effectiveness, and skill development.

This study focused on the role of hope in career advancement but did not look at sources of hope. Participant 8 suggested that when their personal faith was lost, they lost their source of personal hope. Faith was described as a potential source of hope, but further research could examine what a source of hope is and how it operates. Respondents in this study emphasized that hope can be developed. Further research could investigate how hope is most effectively developed, specifically looking at the role of relationships, behaviors, and overcoming and learning from setbacks.

This study did not explore the role of gender, age, or culture in relation to personal hope and success. Future research could study these variables as potential factors in the understanding and demonstration of hope. Also, how pivotal are early in life hope learnings to later in life hope development? There appeared to be a difference in how participants with more professional experience responded versus those with less experience. These potential differences may or may not correlate to age, but further research could explore the relationship of age to hope levels, understanding, and behaviors.

This study did not include demographic data as it was not considered relevant for the purpose of the study. However, there did appear to be a difference in how males and females responded. Gender differences or considerations related to hope could be explored in further research. If context is significant to hope development and demonstration, future research could explore what contexts that support hope might include and what contexts that stifle or prevent hope might include.

Summary

This chapter provided analysis of participant responses. Results indicated that hope can be developed and is positively influenced by supportive contexts and relationships. Also, that it is a leadership responsibility to positively influence hope in their teams through care, empathy, and shared vision and goals. Participants in this study attributed hope development to the experience of overcoming setbacks and learning from them. Results also showed that hope positively influences realizing career goals or outcomes, but career advancement was not a specific career goal provided in this study. These findings could inform how organizational leaders approach career navigation, talent and culture processes, and the development of hope through challenging experiences, supportive relationships, and supportive behaviors.

The research question for this study was: What role did personal hope play in the career advancement of leaders to senior levels in a selected for-profit organization? Participants did not emphasize the role of personal hope in career advancement and did not present career advancement as a primary career goal. Participants described the significance of hope in leadership development and leadership success along the way to career advancement, and indicated that: hope is positively influenced by supportive contexts and relationships, positively influencing hope in others is a leadership responsibility, and hope positively influences realizing career goals.